Cambridge Elements

Elements in Music, 1600–1750
edited by
Rebecca Herissone
University of Manchester
Daniel R. Melamed
Indiana University (Emeritus)

ENGLISH MADRIGALS ON THE JESUIT STAGE

Musical Theatre of Martyrdom at the Venerable English College, Rome

Alana Mailes
University of Southern California

Shaftesbury Road, Cambridge CB2 8EA, United Kingdom

One Liberty Plaza, 20th Floor, New York, NY 10006, USA

477 Williamstown Road, Port Melbourne, VIC 3207, Australia

314–321, 3rd Floor, Plot 3, Splendor Forum, Jasola District Centre, New Delhi – 110025, India

103 Penang Road, #05–06/07, Visioncrest Commercial, Singapore 238467

Cambridge University Press is part of Cambridge University Press & Assessment, a department of the University of Cambridge.

We share the University's mission to contribute to society through the pursuit of education, learning and research at the highest international levels of excellence.

www.cambridge.org
Information on this title: www.cambridge.org/9781009642996

DOI: 10.1017/9781009643016

© Alana Mailes 2025

This publication is in copyright. Subject to statutory exception and to the provisions of relevant collective licensing agreements, no reproduction of any part may take place without the written permission of Cambridge University Press & Assessment.

When citing this work, please include a reference to the DOI 10.1017/9781009643016

First published 2025

A catalogue record for this publication is available from the British Library

ISBN 978-1-009-64299-6 Hardback
ISBN 978-1-009-64297-2 Paperback
ISSN 2755-9726 (online)
ISSN 2755-9718 (print)

Cambridge University Press & Assessment has no responsibility for the persistence or accuracy of URLs for external or third-party internet websites referred to in this publication and does not guarantee that any content on such websites is, or will remain, accurate or appropriate.

For EU product safety concerns, contact us at Calle de José Abascal, 56, 1°, 28003 Madrid, Spain, or email eugpsr@cambridge.org

English Madrigals on the Jesuit Stage

Musical Theatre of Martyrdom at the Venerable English College, Rome

Elements in Music, 1600–1750

DOI: 10.1017/9781009643016
First published online: August 2025

Alana Mailes
University of Southern California
Author for correspondence: Alana Mailes, mailes@usc.edu

Abstract: Throughout the early Stuart period, Catholic seminarians at the Venerable English College, Rome, staged elaborate religious plays for multinational audiences on a nearly annual basis, typically Neo-Latin dramas about martyred English saints. This study shares original archival findings to critically reconstruct the many varieties of music featured in these productions, from French solo song to English madrigals and balletts. This collection of dramatic music includes surviving evidence of English compositions performed in seventeenth-century Italy. The author argues that by embracing foreign musical cultures while also deploying their own musical talents, repertoires, practices, and patronage in service to dramatizations of Catholic martyrdom, this English community was uniquely positioned to build cultural, social, and political connections between Britain and Continental Europe during a significant period of England's rising hegemony in the Mediterranean region and wider world.

Keywords: Madrigal, Rome, English College, Jesuit, theatre

© Alana Mailes 2025

ISBNs: 9781009642996 (HB), 9781009642972 (PB), 9781009643016 (OC)
ISSNs: 2755-9726 (online), 2755-9718 (print)

Contents

1 Introduction — 1

2 Background: Performing English Martyrdom — 5

3 *Thomas Morus*, 1612 — 21

4 *Minutum*, 1613 — 29

5 *Captiva Religio*, 1614 — 42

6 *Roffensis*, 1615 — 49

7 English-Language Plays, 1633–1635 — 51

8 Tragedies by Joseph Simons, 1634–1648 — 57

9 Conclusions — 66

Bibliography — 70

1 Introduction

In the Carnival season of 1614, the English ambassador to Venice, Dudley Carleton, sent diplomatic dispatches to both King James I and the Archbishop of Canterbury, describing, of all things, a school play. Carleton complained to the archbishop George Abbot, "[Y]^r L^p will have heard how the colledge of English Jesuits at Rome entertained all spectators wth a ridiculous tragidie of theyr owne countrie ... uppon the old theme of persequution wherin they doe exceedingly tempt his Maties clemency to turne fictas in Veras tragedias wch they worthely desearve."[1] This "ridiculous tragidie" was the Latin tragicomedy *Captiva Religio* (author unknown), which had just been performed at the Venerable English College in Rome and portrayed the maltreatment of Catholics in Protestant England.[2] Carleton reported to the king that the play had been staged more than once, "first before the Cardinal [Odoardo] Farnese (protector of the English fugitives) and some other Cardinals and chiefe prelats, and after more publiquely, wth liberty for all spectators."[3] *Captiva* was only one of many theatrical productions about anti-Catholic persecution presented at the English College in the seventeenth century. These plays showcased a wide variety of vocal and instrumental music, which in *Captiva* alone ranged from a pantomime satyr dance and a French folk tune to a sacred Italian piece played on the viol. Carleton rarely discussed the theatre in his correspondences, but *Captiva* was clearly newsworthy. The ambassador understood, as surely did his two readers, that English Jesuit drama possessed a geopolitical power that needed to be monitored.

The Venerable English College, Rome, was founded in 1579 to train English secular clergy to reconvert post-Reformation Britain to the Catholic faith. Though the English College was not constitutionally Jesuit, it was placed under administration of the English and Welsh Jesuit mission and so operated much like a Jesuit institution. Throughout the Tudor and early Stuart periods, persecuted English Catholics found safe haven at the college (henceforth the VEC), but many of those students ventured to Rome in preparation to one day travel back across the English Channel on dangerous underground proselytizing missions, for which they would risk torture and execution by the English government. Capital punishment of recusants dwindled under James I, but for many English Catholics in Britain, a grisly death sentence remained a real

---

[1] Dudley Carleton to George Abbot, February 28, 1614, State Papers 99/15, f. 98r, The National Archives, London (henceforth cited as TNA). See also Carleton to James I, February 11, 1614, State Papers 99/15, ff. 83r–86r, TNA.

[2] See M. Wiggins and C. Richardson, "1741. Captiva [The Female Captive]" in *British Drama 1533–1642: A Catalogue*, Vol. 6 (Oxford: Oxford University Press, 2015).

[3] Carleton to James I, February 11, 1614, State Papers 99/15, f. 83r, TNA.

possibility. The seminary, located on Via di Monserrato since its founding, therefore grew into an international center for veneration of the Catholic martyr, which was promoted by the institution's thriving musical and theatrical culture.[4]

In the first half of the seventeenth century, VEC students staged elaborate religious plays at the college on a nearly annual basis, typically during the final weeks of Carnival. The college's plays, in accordance with Jesuit regulations, almost always were spoken in Latin, omitted women characters, and dealt with sacred subjects, usually the lives of famous English Catholic martyrs. Students of various ages were cast as actors, and payments for props, costumes, scenery, and music were made by the college and its individual lodgers. For plays with extensive scenery and machinery, students would erect a temporary stage in the college's spacious *salone*, located over the refectory. Audiences for these dramas became so large that plays were given repeat performances as many as five times, and the college often required the assistance of papal Swiss Guards for crowd management. A typical audience consisted of roughly three-hundred people, over a dozen of whom would have been cardinals invited as guests of honor.[5] These shows were a major cultural attraction in Seicento Rome, presenting a very specific image of the "English nation" and its music to the wider world.

Several scholars have produced critical editions and literary analyses of various Neo-Latin dramatic texts that were acted at the college, and a few authors have provided slight information about the music featured in these productions. Suzanne Gossett published the first and only detailed article about drama at the college, which exhumed long-lost information about musicians and instruments derived from VEC account books; Marie-Anne de Kisch shared that some VEC theatrical sources contain music by the English organist, composer, and music theorist Thomas Morley (1557–1602); and Dana Sutton has made modern translated editions of nearly all known VEC plays, with notes on music.[6] Nonetheless, there remains a general scarcity of research on all

---

[4] For the college as a center of Catholic martyrdom, see A. Dillon, *The Construction of Martyrdom in the English Catholic Community, 1535–1603* (London: Routledge, 2002), 170–242; C. M. Richardson, "Durante Alberti, the *Martyrs' Picture* and the Venerable English College, Rome," *Papers of the British School at Rome* 73 (2005): 223–63; L. Underwood, "Representing England in Rome: Sermons from the Early Modern English College to Popes and Cardinals," *Reformation & Renaissance Review* 23 (2021): 4–26; and R. L. Williams, "Ancient Bodies and Contested Identities in the English College Martyrdom Cycle, Rome," in A. Hopkins and M. Wyke (eds.), *Roman Bodies: Antiquity to the Eighteenth Century* (London: The British School at Rome, 2005), 185–200.

[5] S. Gossett, "Drama in the English College, Rome, 1591–1660," *English Literary Renaissance* 3, no. 1 (1973): 60–93.

[6] For studies on musical drama at the college, see Gossett, "Drama in the English College, Rome, 1591–1660" and "English Plays in the English College Archives," *The Venerabile* 28, no. 1 (1983): 23–33; M. de Kisch, "A propos de Huit Pièces Inédites (1612–1614) dans les Archives du

musical life at the VEC in this period, and the college's theatrical music has hitherto never been critically analyzed. The music made and heard in these productions, however, was more than a mere decoration: It was a fundamental component of the seminary's dramatic martyrology.

Theatre historians have recognized that the college's dramatic texts compounded literary traditions variously associated with Continental Jesuit school drama, English university theatre, and English and Italian public theatre, but the music in these plays also demonstrates its own transcultural complexity. The VEC's Roman and other foreign audiences heard English historical fiction acted and sung in Latin, interspersed with Italian, French, and English (including Italianate English) music and featuring the instrumental and vocal talents of English seminarians and professional musicians employed elsewhere in Rome, including at Saint Peter's Basilica. These musicians played many different instruments either owned by the college's residents or rented from other nearby institutions.[7] The VEC was unique from other English colleges abroad in its regular hire of papal musical talent, its high concentration of vitriolic anti-Protestant martyr plays, and its repeated inclusion of a popular Italian musico-dramatic form, the *intermedio*.[8] Nowhere else in the world did these diverse cultural influences come together to recurrently venerate the Catholic martyr.

I have consulted printed plays and seventeenth-century manuscript sources held in the VEC archives, Vatican Library, and British State Papers to critically reconstruct dramatic music at the college in the early Stuart period. In sharing

---

Collège Anglais de Rome," *Études Anglaises, Grande Bretagne-Ètats-Unis* 25 (1972): 525–9 and "Fêtes et représentations au Collège Anglais de Rome 1612–1614" in J. Jacquot and E. Konigson (eds.), *Les Fêtes de la Renaissance* (Paris: Editions du Centre national de la recherche scientifique, 1975), 525–43; W. H. McCabe, *An Introduction to the Jesuit Theater: A Posthumous Work*, ed. L. J. Oldani (Saint Louis: Institute of Jesuit Sources, 1983); H. B. Norland, "Political Martyrdom at the English College in Rome" in J. Bloemendal and N. Smith (eds.), *Politics and Aesthetics in European Baroque and Classicist Tragedy* (Leiden: Brill, 2016), 135–51; A. Shell, *Catholicism, Controversy and the English Literary Imagination, 1558–1660* (Cambridge: Cambridge University Press, 2004), 169–223; and D. Sutton, "English Jesuit Drama in the Sixteenth and Seventeenth Centuries," *Oxford Handbooks* (2013), https://doi.org/10.1093/oxfordhb/9780199935338.013.003.

[7] See Gossett, "Drama in the English College, Rome, 1591–1660," 78–80.

[8] Sutton, "English Jesuit Drama in the Sixteenth and Seventeenth Centuries." For the *intermedio* at the VEC and elsewhere in Rome, see F. Hammond, *Music & Spectacle in Baroque Rome: Barberini Patronage under Urban VIII* (New Haven: Yale University Press, 1994); V. C. Lamothe, "The Theater of Piety: Sacred Operas for the Barberini Family (Rome, 1632–1643)," unpublished Ph.D. diss., University of North Carolina at Chapel Hill (2009); and M. Murata, "Dal ridicolo al diletto signorile. Rospigliosi and the Intermedio in Rome" in G. Giron-Panel and A. Goulet (eds.), *La Musique à Rome au xviie siècle: Études et perspectives de recherche* (Rome: Publications de l'École française de Rome, 2012), 269–89, "Opera as Spectacle, Opera as Drama" in J. Weber (ed.), *The Cambridge Companion to Seventeenth-Century Opera* (Cambridge: Cambridge University Press, 2021), 77–101, and *Operas for the Papal Court, 1631–1668* (Ann Arbor: UMI Research Press, 1981).

these new findings, this study identifies the college's theatre program as a key setting for musical exchange between Britain and Continental Europe in the early modern period. Moreover, this research on theatrical music at the college defies traditional music-historical narratives about a unidirectional importation of Italian music and musicians into early modern England. The VEC archives contain, as far as I am aware, the only surviving evidence of English musical repertoires performed for foreign listeners in seventeenth-century Italy.

Following a general introduction to the VEC and its theatre program, I present all records that I have gathered of music featured or discussed in early Seicento VEC plays, considering the various dramatic functions that this music served on-stage and how it might have represented English cultural and national identity to its audiences. I provide informed speculation about how this music might have been performed on the VEC stage, and I explore the relationship in each college production between English and other, Continental musical influences, focusing especially on VEC performances of Italianate madrigal and ballett repertoires. I illustrate how music making and discussion of music in college plays stressed the sanctity of Catholic and Catholic-coded martyrs in sharp contrast to their heretical adversaries by thematically and sonically drawing associations between Englishness, Italo-Catholic musicality, and transnational Catholic piety.

I begin by surveying four anonymously authored Neo-Latin martyr dramas: *Thomas Morus* (1612), the *intermedio Minutum* first performed during the play *Sanctus Thomas Cantuariensis* (1613), *Captiva Religio* (1614), and *Roffensis* (1615). I then examine two English-language plays on secular themes, also of unknown authorship, staged at the college during the Caroline period: *The New Moon* (1633) and *Comedy of Geometry* (c. 1635). This study concludes with an analysis of music in three dramas written by the Jesuit priest and playwright Joseph Simons (alias Emmanuel Lobb, 1594–1671), who became rector of the college in the 1650s: *Zeno* (1634), *Leo Armenus* (a.k.a. *Ultio divina*, 1645), and *Mercia* (1648).

I argue that by embracing foreign musical cultures while also deploying their own musical talents, repertoires, practices, and patronage in service to the Catholic martyr's cause, this English community was uniquely positioned to build cultural, social, and political connections between Britain and the Continent at a historical moment in which the expansion of England's nascent global empire depended upon heightened British interaction with Catholic Europe and the Mediterranean world more broadly. Through compelling musico-dramatic depictions of Catholic martyrdom, VEC seminarians laid claim to a substantial role within the global Jesuit martyrology, thereby affirming their presence within the Church and city of Rome, eliciting international sympathy for persecuted English Catholics, and asserting control over the English historical narrative abroad by projecting an image of England as a nation rooted in a rich Catholic religious history and Italo-Catholic musical culture.

Retaining a familiarity with English musical repertoires would have equipped seminarians for social reintegration upon their eventual return missions to Britain, where Catholic clergy had to covertly evangelize in private domestic spaces; some priests even disguised themselves as household music teachers.[9] Cultural accommodation – and, in this instance, cultural reassimilation – was central to the Jesuit conversion strategy on a global scale.[10] At the same time, by assimilating into Roman theatrical culture, a highly visible exemplar of transnational exchange, the college's theatre program conveyed to its audiences England's continued participation in and contributions to the broader musical culture of Catholic Europe. The VEC theatre's musical activity was a vehicle for the growth of English cosmopolitanism in an age of English nation building and imperial expansion, facilitating England's cultural ascension onto the world stage.

2 Background: Performing English Martyrdom

From its earliest days as the medieval Hospice of the Most Holy Trinity and Saint Thomas, the English College had been a place of refuge for English and Welsh pilgrims in Rome. During the reign of Queen Elizabeth I (1558–1603), however, the hospice assumed a new, immensely politicized identity. The institution was converted by, among others, the English Cardinal William Allen (1532–94) into a seminary for English and Welsh Catholics, confirmed with a bull of foundation issued in 1579 by Pope Gregory XIII. The VEC was to employ Jesuit priests to educate at least forty students at a time, most above eighteen years of age, in theology, philosophy, and ancient languages, principally to equip a legion of missionary priests to reconvert post-Reformation Britain to Catholicism. In the early seventeenth century, the college continued to operate as a haven of hospitality and charity, but it had also become a training

---

[9] For newer work on English Jesuit conversion through music, see J. Flynn, "English Jesuit Missionaries, Music Education, and the Musical Participation of Women in Devotional Life in Recusant Households from ca. 1580–1630," in L. P. Austern, C. Bailey, and A. E. Winkler (eds.), *Beyond Boundaries: Rethinking Music Circulation in Early Modern England* (Bloomington: Indiana University Press, 2017), 29–41; and E. K. M. Murphy, "Music and Catholic Culture in Post-Reformation Lancashire: Piety, Protest, and Conversion," *British Catholic History* 32, no. 4 (2015): 492–525.

[10] For a general introduction to Jesuit music and cultural accommodation, see D. R. M. Irving, "Music in Global Jesuit Missions, 1540–1773," in I. G. Županov (ed.), *The Oxford Handbook of the Jesuits* (New York: Oxford University Press, 2019), 598–634.

ground for future British priests, a boarding school for British Catholic laity, the headquarters of the English and Welsh Jesuit mission, and an internationally renowned site for the veneration of Catholic martyrs. While resident at the nearby Hospital of San Girolamo della Carità, Saint Philip Neri (1515–95), the Italian priest and founder of the eponymous Oratory, would greet VEC scholars by singing the martyr hymn *Salvete flores martyrum*.[11]

The VEC's reputation as an international center for martyrdom was supported by the college's rich, multifaceted culture of performance and music making. Beyond practicing the more inward devotional Spiritual Exercises of the Society of Jesus, VEC scholars participated in processions and pilgrimages, preached in the college church and papal chapel, and presented public academic orations, some with musical interludes.[12] Students received instruction at the college in singing and diverse instruments. The VEC was home to a thriving chapel music establishment based in the college Church of the Most Holy Trinity and St. Thomas. The college chapel employed many eminent musicians, notably the part-time *maestro di cappella* and composer Virgilio Mazzocchi (1597–1646), who also taught at the Roman Seminary and advanced to the position of chapelmaster at San Pietro.[13] Two well-known English Catholic organists and composers also took on musical duties at the college: Peter Philips (c. 1560–1628) in 1582–5 and Richard Dering (c. 1580–1630) in 1612–15. According to newly discovered VEC and other Jesuit documents, Dering was appointed vice-prefect of music and eventually served as *maestro di cappella*. It is possible that Dering directed or was at least involved in the college theatre program during his sojourn in Rome, although he probably arrived after the 1612 VEC performance of *Thomas Morus*. The composer and violist Henry Butler (d. 1652), also visited the college more than once: 1613–17 and again in 1648–9.[14]

---

[11] For the VEC's early history, see M. E. Williams, *The Venerable English College, Rome: A History* (Leominster: Gracewing, 2008). See also P. F. Grendler, *Jesuit Schools and Universities in Europe, 1548–1773* (Leiden: Brill, 2018), 1–27.

[12] See G. Jakovac, "Performance Culture at the English College in Rome, c. 1579–1660," in M. Binasco (ed.), *The English Community of Rome, 1500–1829* (Brill, forthcoming in 2025).

[13] See G. Dixon, "Music in the Venerable English College in the Early Baroque" in B. M. Antolini, A. Morelli, and V. V. Spagnuolo (eds.), *La musica a Roma attraverso le fonti d'archivio: Atti del Convegno internazionale Roma 4–7 giugno 1992* (Lucca: Libreria Musicale Italiana, 1994), 469–78; and Murata, "*Dal ridicolo al diletto signorile*," "Opera as Spectacle, Opera as Drama," and *Operas for the Papal Court 1631–1668*.

[14] For Philips at the VEC, see R. Taylor, "Peter Philips (1560/1561–1628) and the Venerable English College, Rome," in B. Bouckaert and E. Schreurs (eds.), *The Di Martinelli Music Collection (KULeuven, University Archives): Musical Life in Collegiate Churches in the Low Countries and Europe: Chant and Polyphony* (Leuven: Alamire, 2000), 243–60. For Dering's conversion and musical activity at the VEC, see my "A Stuart Musician's Conversion to Catholicism: Richard Dering and the Venerable English College, Rome" (co-authored with Maurice Whitehead), *Music & Letters* 106, no. 1 (2025): 1–28.

Musical VEC services are known to have drawn sympathetic crowds, especially on the annual feast day of the college's martyred medieval patron saint. Patronal feast days became elaborate public events, in which professional ensembles of talented local singers and instrumentalists were hired to bolster the college's chapel music. Some musicians were even compelled to offer their services to the college *gratis*. Whenever seminarians received news that an English priest, namely any college alumnus, had been executed in England, they would gather together in the chapel to sing the *Te Deum laudamus* hymn in memory of the deceased. From the 1580s onward, this chapel was decorated with a fresco cycle by Niccolò Circignani that graphically illustrated the violent martyrdoms of numerous English and Welsh saints. The chapel also featured an altarpiece by Durante Alberti, *The Martyrs' Picture*, which depicted the martyred English Saints Thomas of Canterbury and Edmund of East Anglia.[15]

For early modern Jesuit missionaries worldwide, martyrdom was valorized as the highest form of Christ-like self-sacrifice, a prize to be won and a rite of spiritual possession over missionized and colonized territories. It could even be welcomed as an expected backlash when Indigenous communities revolted against violence inflicted upon them by the society.[16] Jesuit school plays performed everywhere from Japan to New Spain told countless blood-soaked tales of Catholic martyrdom.[17] Although most other Jesuit institutions in and

---

[15] For further scholarship on the VEC chapel and the college as a cultural center for the Catholic martyr, see Dillon, *The Construction of Martyrdom in the English Catholic Community, 1535–1603*, 170–242; Dixon, "Music in the Venerable English College in the Early Baroque"; E. K. M. Murphy, "Music and Post-Reformation English Catholics: Place, Sociability, and Space, 1570–1640," unpublished Ph.D. diss., University of York (2014), 18–32, 70–8, 238–42, and "Musical Self-Fashioning and the 'Theatre of Death' in Late Elizabethan and Jacobean England," *Renaissance Studies* 30, no. 3 (2015): 410–29; Richardson, "Durante Alberti, the *Martyrs' Picture* and the Venerable English College, Rome"; Underwood, "Representing England in Rome"; and Williams, "Ancient Bodies and Contested Identities in the English College Martyrdom Cycle, Rome."

[16] For recent work on global Jesuit martyrdom, see B. Bayne, *Missions Begin with Blood: Suffering and Salvation in the Borderlands of New Spain* (New York: Fordham University Press, 2022); A. Cañeque, "Iberian Imperial Rivalries and the Missionary Conquest of Japan," in R. C. Casal and C. Egan (eds.), *The Routledge Hispanic Studies Companion to Early Modern Spanish Literature and Culture* (London: Routledge, 2022), 47–60, and "In the Shadow of Francis Xavier: Martyrdom and Colonialism in the Jesuit Asian Missions," *Journal of Jesuit Studies* 9 (2022): 438–58; and F. A. L. de Carvalho, *Missionizing on the Edge: Religion and Power in the Jesuit Missions of Spanish Amazonia* (Leiden: Brill, 2023).

[17] For recent scholarship on global Jesuit martyr drama, see A. S. Keener, "Japan Dramas and Shakespeare at St. Omers English Jesuit College," *Renaissance Quarterly* 74 (2021): 876–917; S. Kirk, "Relics, Jesuit Masculinity, and the Performance of Martyrdom in *Triumpho de los Sanctos*," *Latin American Theatre Review* 54, no. 1 (2020): 79–98; H. Oba, A. Watanabe, and F. Schaffenrath (eds.), *Japan on the Jesuit Stage: Transmissions, Receptions, and Regional Contexts* (Leiden: Brill, 2022); and M. H. Takao, "'In What Storms of Blood from Christ's Flock is Japan Swimming?': Gratia Hosokawa and the Performative Representation of Japanese Martyrdom in *Mulier fortis* (1698)," in Y. Haskell and R. Garrod (eds.), *Changing Hearts:*

out of Rome presented a variety of Catholic historical and morality plays without exclusively concentrating on martyrdom, martyrological iconography, devotion, and drama were ubiquitous throughout Counter-Reformation Italy.[18] The VEC tapped into a far-reaching cultural fixation on the Catholic martyr at a time when the canonization and veneration of martyred saints had been invigorated worldwide and the city of Rome had transformed into the capital of the global Catholic church, widely regarded as the first world religion.[19]

At its core, Jesuit musical theatre was an autodidactic exercise that instilled in seminarians moral and theological doctrine as well as many linguistic, rhetorical, oratorical, and memorization skills necessary for Catholic evangelization.[20] According to some early modern commentators, music in Jesuit theatre was also meant to move the affections of spectator-auditors, inspiring their own spiritual transformation in response to what audiences saw and heard on-stage.[21] Andrew Cichy and Emilie Murphy have examined how English Catholic identity was shaped through musical praxis in English colleges and convents in foreign locales such as Douai, Brussels, Valladolid, and, most pertinent to this study, Rome. They have detailed how both secular and sacred musicking in these institutions operated as a mode of martyrological self-fashioning. Participation in music transformed seminarians into public icons of Catholic martyrdom and prepared them to forge ahead with the English Catholic mission, even if their clandestine conversion efforts in Britain were destined to end in death.[22]

Performing Jesuit Emotions between Europe, Asia, and the Americas (Leiden: Brill, 2019), 87–120.

[18] See Hammond, *Music & Spectacle in Baroque Rome*, 37–42; R. L. Kendrick, "Martyrdom in Seventeenth-Century Italian Music" in P. M. Jones and T. Worcester (eds.), *From Rome to Eternity: Catholicism and the Arts in Italy, ca. 1550–1650*, (Leiden: Brill, 2002), 121–41; Lamothe, "Theater of Piety"; and L. J. Oldani and V. R. Yanitelli, "Jesuit Theater in Italy: Its Entrances and Exit," *Italica* 76, no. 1 (1999): 18–32.

[19] S. Ditchfield, "*Romanus* and *Catholicus*: Counter-Reformation Rome as *Caput Mundi*," 131–47, and Pamela M. Jones, "Celebrating New Saints in Rome and across the Globe," 148–66, in P. M. Jones, B. Wisch, and S. Ditchfield (eds.), *A Companion to Early Modern Rome, 1492–1692* (Leiden: Brill, 2019). See also Kendrick, "Martyrdom in Seventeenth-Century Italian Music."

[20] See R. S. Miola, "Jesuit Drama in Early Modern England," in R. Dutton, A. Findlay, and R. Wilson (eds.), *Theatre and Religion: Lancastrian Shakespeare* (Manchester: Manchester University Press, 2003), 71–86; H. B. Norland, "Neo-Latin Drama in Britain," in J. Bloemendal and Norland (eds.), *Neo-Latin Drama and Theatre in Early Modern Europe* (Leiden: Brill, 2013), 471–544; Oldani and Yanitelli, "Jesuit Theater in Italy"; A. Shell, "Autodidacticism in English Jesuit Drama: The Writings and Career of Joseph Simons," *Medieval & Renaissance Drama in England* 13 (2001): 34–56; and Sutton, "English Jesuit Drama in the Sixteenth and Seventeenth Centuries."

[21] Takao, "In What Storms of Blood from Christ's Flock is Japan Swimming?" 103–4.

[22] See A. Cichy, "'How Shall We Sing the Song of the Lord in a Strange Land?' English Catholic Music after the Reformation to 1700: A Study of Institutions in Continental Europe," unpublished D.Phil. thesis, University of Oxford (2013) and "Music, Meditation, and Martyrdom in a Seventeenth-Century English Seminary," *Music & Letters* 97, no. 2 (2016): 205–20; Murphy,

Musicking in English colleges abroad was not only a weapon of spiritual warfare, however. It was also an effective means by which English students ingratiated themselves with their foreign hosts, as it stimulated personal interaction and artistic exchange across cultures. At the heart of this music making laid a paradox: English seminarians strove to musically assimilate to their surroundings while also distinguishing themselves within the Counter-Reformation musical establishment as markedly English exemplars of Catholic missionary zeal.[23] As this study will suggest, it was precisely this cultural tension that seems to have so captivatingly animated the VEC's musical theatre program for audiences in Rome. As scholars such as Valeria de Lucca, José María Domínguez, Anne-Madeleine Goulet, Margaret Murata, and Èlodie Oriel have established, seventeenth-century Roman theatrical culture was a competitive arena in which rival patrons financed musical drama as an image-building enterprise. In supporting local performances of plays and operas, patrons strove to project targeted, strategic constructions of their own public personas.[24] Out of this great flurry of musico-dramatic activity in Rome, the VEC emerged as a leading theatrical institution that promoted its own particular image of English identity as a Catholic religiosity that was both distinctive and cosmopolitan.

I read the VEC's musical theatre of martyrdom as just one means by which the confessional mobility – to borrow the term coined by Liesbeth Corens – of English Catholics across the Channel furthered the global ambitions of the

---

"Musical Self-Fashioning and the 'Theatre of Death' in Late Elizabethan and Jacobean England" and "Music and Post-Reformation English Catholics."

[23] See Cichy, "'Changing Their Tune': Sacred Music and the Recasting of English Post-Reformation Identity at St. Alban's College, Valladolid," in D. Filippi and M. J. Noone (eds.), *Listening to Early Modern Catholicism: Perspectives from Musicology* (Leiden: Brill, 2017), 173–86, "'How Shall We Sing the Song of the Lord in a Strange Land?' English Catholic Music after the Reformation to 1700," and "Music, Meditation, and Martyrdom in a Seventeenth-Century English Seminary"; and E. K. M. Murphy, "A Sense of Place: Hearing English Catholicism in the Spanish Habsburg Territories, 1568–1659," in R. MacDonald, Murphy, and E. L. Swann (eds.), *Sensing the Sacred in Medieval and Early Modern Culture* (London: Routledge, 2018), 136–57, "Music and Post-Reformation English Catholics," and "Musical Self-Fashioning and the 'Theatre of Death' in Late Elizabethan and Jacobean England." For this same paradox in VEC sermons, see Underwood, "Representing England in Rome."

[24] See V. de Lucca, "Patronage" in H. M. Greenwald (ed.), *The Oxford Handbook of Opera* (Oxford: Oxford University Press, 2014), 648–65, and *The Politics of Princely Entertainment: Music and Spectacle in the Lives of Lorenzo Onofrio and Maria Mancini Colonna* (Oxford: Oxford University Press, 2020); A. Goulet, J. M. Dominguez, and E. Oriel (eds.), *Spectacles et performances artistiques à Rome (1644–1740): Une analyse historique à partir des archives familiales de l'aristocratie* (Rome: Publications de l'École française de Rome, 2021), https://doi.org/10.4000/books.efr.16344; Lamothe, "Theater of Piety"; and Murata "Opera as Spectacle, Opera as Drama" and *"Theatri intra theatrum* or, the Church and the Stage in Seventeenth-Century Rome" in K. K. Forney (ed.), *Sleuthing the Muse: Essays in Honor of William Prizer* (New York: Pendragon Press, 2012), 181–200.

society and Counter-Reformation Church, elevating budding conceptions of English nationhood to a place of prominence within the cultural life of Catholic Europe.[25] Specifically on the topic of martyrdom, Richard Williams has argued that the college chapel's cycle of martyr murals promoted a favorable view of English national identity in Rome by emphasizing a portrayal of England as home to an enduring Orthodox Catholic history.[26] Lucy Underwood has similarly asserted that VEC sermons turned to themes of martyrdom both to situate the institution within the unified global papal Church and to distinguish English Catholic sanctity as unique.[27] Notwithstanding its Roman headquarters and accused disloyalty to the Crown, the English mission was still a patriotic project, one that relied on financial support from public alms, the papacy, and wealthy private patrons, domestic and foreign.[28] My work is informed by these critical perspectives on English nation and martyrdom and also by an expanding musicological literature exploring how early modern nationality was produced through musical expression of collective belonging in Roman national religious institutions, a process of identity construction that relied at once on cultural assimilation into Roman festive models and assertions of national singularity.[29]

My use of the descriptor "English" rather than "British" is never motivated by a wish to overlook "Britishness" as an incipient political identity arising from the Stuart Union of the Crowns. Rather, I have chosen this terminology to stress England's position within unequal British structures of governance and also in reference to the VEC community's own theorization of English identity as set apart from other ethnic groups within Britain on the basis of both perceived cultural difference and fictions of a shared Saxon heritage cutting across

---

[25] For the interpretive model of confessional mobility as recently developed by L. Corens, see Corens, *Confessional Mobility and English Catholics in Counter-Reformation Europe* (Oxford: Oxford University Press, 2019). For recent work on the formation of English nationhood at the VEC, see B. Lockey, "Catholics and Cosmopolitans Writing the Nation: The Pope's Scholars and the 1579 Student Rebellion at the English Roman College" in B. Fuchs and E. Weissbourd (eds.), *Representing Imperial Rivalry in the Early Modern Mediterranean* (Toronto: University of Toronto Press, 2015), 233–54, and *Early Modern Catholics, Royalists, and Cosmopolitans: English Transnationalism and the Christian Commonwealth* (London: Routledge, 2016); and M. Netzloff, "The English Colleges and the English Nation: Allen, Persons, Verstegan, and Diasporic Nationalism" in R. Corthell, F. Dolan, C. Highley, and A. F. Marotti (eds.), *Catholic Culture in Early Modern England* (Indiana: University of Notre Dame Press, 2007), 236–60.

[26] Williams, "Ancient Bodies and Contested Identities in the English College Martyrdom Cycle, Rome."

[27] Underwood, "Representing England in Rome."

[28] For VEC finances, see T. M. McCoog, "'The Slightest Suspicion of Avarice': The Finances of the English Jesuit Mission," *Recusant History* 19, no. 2 (1988): 103–23.

[29] See M. Berti, E. Corswarem, and J. Morales (eds.), *Music and the Identity Process: The National Churches of Rome and their Networks in the Early Modern Period* (Turnhout: Brepols, 2019); and V. de Lucca and C. Jeanneret (eds.), *The Grand Theater of the World: Music, Space, and the Performance of Identity in Early Modern Rome* (London: Routledge, 2019).

confessional divisions. Most glaringly, VEC seminarians in the late sixteenth century rebelled against the college's Welsh rector, Maurice Clenock, and expelled the institution's Welsh students.[30] Separate Scots and Irish Colleges were also founded in Rome in 1600 and 1625, respectively. In some cases, I do deliberately use the terms "British" and "Britain" as geographical signifiers so as to not exclude Scotland and Wales from consideration.

In analyzing cultural formations of English nationhood in Rome, it is also important to consider that the VEC ascended to a prominent position in Roman theatrical culture during a critical period of rising English hegemony in Mediterranean trade and the colonial world. As Maria Fusaro has detailed, England's global commercial successes resulted in large part from British economic enterprises in Italy and emulation of Venetian commercial and cultural practices.[31] Alison Games has also shown how an early modern uptick in English travel abroad, for example on the "Grand Tour" of Italy, and the resultant cultivation of English cosmopolitanism ultimately enabled the emergence of the British Empire. English Catholics played a notable role in this history, not only as travelers in Catholic lands but also as colonial proprietors; the North American colony of Maryland, for example, was established in 1632 under the Catholic Cecil Calvert and English Jesuit leadership.[32] As is narrated in most traditional histories of English music, the Tudor and Stuart periods saw a vogue for Italian music in Britain, much of it exported from a rival maritime trading empire, the Republic of Venice. My ongoing research on early modern Anglo-Italian musical exchange reexamines this "Italianization" of English music as a form of inter-imperial mimesis.[33] While the present study does not

---

[30] See Lockey, "Catholics and Cosmopolitans Writing the Nation" and *Early Modern Catholics, Royalists, and Cosmopolitans*.

[31] M. Fusaro, *Political Economies of Empire in the Early Modern Mediterranean: The Decline of Venice and the Rise of England, 1450–1700* (Cambridge: Cambridge University Press, 2015).

[32] See A. Games, *The Web of Empire: English Cosmopolitans in an Age of Expansion, 1560–1660* (Oxford: Oxford University Press, 2008). For recent scholarship on the early Catholic history of Maryland, see M. D. Breidenbach, *Our Dear-Bought Liberty: Catholics and Religious Toleration in Early America* (Cambridge, MA: Harvard University Press, 2021); R. E. Curran, *Papist Devils: Catholics in British America, 1574–1783* (Washington, DC: The Catholic University of America Press, 2014); C. W. Gollar, *"Let Us Go Free": Slavery and Jesuit Universities in America* (Washington, DC: Georgetown University Press, 2024); L. E. Masur, "Plantation as Mission: American Indians, Enslaved Africans, and Jesuit Missionaries in Maryland," *Journal of Jesuit Studies* 8 (2021): 385–407; C. O'Donnell, *Jesuits in the North American Colonies and the United States: Faith, Conflict, Adaptation*. (Leiden: Brill, 2020); and A. Sutto, *Loyal Protestants & Dangerous Papists: Maryland and the Politics of Religion in the English Atlantic, 1630–1690* (Virginia: University of Virginia Press, 2015).

[33] This will be explicated in my current book project on musical and diplomatic exchange between England and Seicento Venice. For inter-imperial mimesis, see J. Adelman, "Mimesis and Rivalry: European Empires and Global Regimes," *Journal of Global History* 10, no. 1 (2015): 77–98; B. Fuchs, *Mimesis and Empire: The New World, Islam, and European Identities* (Cambridge: Cambridge University Press, 2001); Fuchs and Weissbourd (eds.),

aim to investigate such dimensions of Anglo-Roman musical interactions, the VEC theatre's projections of English nation and cosmopolitanism were unquestionably underpinned by this complex geopolitical context and so must be studied in conversation with music scholarship on the global movements of missionaries, merchants, colonists, and other agents of empire.[34]

A veritable "theatre of the world," Seicento Rome was a dynamic international hub of dramatic music and spectacle, especially in the Carnival season. Jesuit school theatre abounded, and elite families such as the Barberini and Rospigliosi sponsored the production of operas and other musical dramas often composed and performed by the same musicians who worked at institutions such as the English College, German College, and Roman Seminary. What is more, many of the same eminent diplomats, aristocrats, monarchs, and clerics who attended papal musico-dramatic productions also attended student shows at seminaries. Jesuit theatre was instrumental to the development of musical drama throughout and beyond early modern Europe, particularly in Rome, considering the region's high concentration of Jesuit schools, recurrent papal bans on other plays containing secular subject matter, and lack of public theatres relative to other Italian city-states such as Venice.[35] In seventeenth-century Rome, it was standard fare for musical *intermedi* to be performed between the acts of plays and in public ceremonies, including Jesuit school dramas and academic orations. The *intermedio* was itself integral to the rise of Italian opera. Student *intermedi* in Rome departed from most other *intermedio* practices in the peninsula by acting out schoolboy jokes and pranks.[36] No music survives for most early Roman

---

Representing Imperial Rivalry in the Early Modern Mediterranean; and R. Roque, "Mimesis and Colonialism: Emerging Perspectives on a Shared History," *History Compass* 13, no. 4 (2015): 201–11.

[34] For a recent collection of scholarship in this area, see E. Wilbourne and S. G. Cusick (eds.), *Acoustemologies in Contact: Sounding Subjects and Modes of Listening in Early Modernity* (Cambridge: Open Book, 2021).

[35] For general introductions to musical theatre in Seicento Rome, see de Lucca, *The Politics of Princely Entertainment*; Goulet, Dominguez, and Oriel (eds.), *Spectacles et performances artistiques à Rome (1644–1740)*; D. Kimbell, *Italian Opera* (Cambridge: Cambridge University Press, 1991), 97–113; S. Leopold, "Rome: Sacred and Secular," in Curtis Price (ed.), *The Early Baroque Era: From the Late 16th Century to the 1660s* (Basingstoke: Macmillan, 1993), 49–74; and Murata "Opera as Spectacle, Opera as Drama" and "*Theatri intra theatrum.*" For recent work on Jesuit musical drama in Rome beyond the VEC, see, for example, A. V. Clark, "Carissimi's *Jephte* and Jesuit Spirituality," *College Music Symposium* 59, no. 1 (2019): 1–33; E. L. Lyon, "'Magis corde quam organo': Agazzari, Amadino, and the Hidden Meanings of *Eumelio*," *Early Music* 48, no. 2 (2020): 156–76; and A. Roma,"'Per allevare li giovani nel timor di Dio e nelle lettere': Arti performative, educazione e controllo al Collegio Nazareno di Roma nel primo Seicento," in Goulet, Dominguez, and Oriel (eds.), *Spectacles et performances artistiche à Rome (1644–1740)*.

[36] See Murata, "*Dal ridicolo al diletto signorile.*"

intermedi, but it is known that from the late 1620s, much of their music at the Roman and Vatican Seminaries was composed by Mazzocchi. Roman *intermedi* usually featured madrigals and closely related dance genres such as the *balletto*, a practice which the VEC stage evidently followed.[37]

The earliest known English College plays were acted in the 1590s. There followed a long pause in musico-dramatic activity at the VEC under the rectorship of Robert Persons, probably both a financial decision and an effort to cultivate a less indulgent public image for the college. Musical theatre at the VEC was vigorously revived during the rectorship of Thomas Owen (1610–18), whose support for music and drama at the college clearly represents a differing vision for the institution. Revitalized patronage of music and theatre supported Owen's position as prefect of the English and Welsh Jesuit mission, which saw an enormous growth in the society's numbers under the Superior General Claudio Acquaviva, as well as the VEC's budding role as an educational center for future Catholic lay leadership in England. This influx of predominantly self-funded highborn students, known as "convictors," appears to have prompted a hearty revival of the college's musical and dramatic activity.[38]

The VEC continued to present plays throughout the 1640s when the Civil War had forced the closure of theatres in England. Although many college plays were performed in Latin on sacred subjects, the VEC and other Jesuit theatre programs did occasionally stage vernacular dramas on secular subjects. It is plausible that VEC English-language dramas were reserved for a minority of spectator-auditors who could understand the show's dialogue. By 1633 the college's dramatic culture had begun to change, distancing itself from overt anti-Protestant sentiment and confessionalization as a thematic focus. Religious persecution in England had relaxed under the Stuarts, especially once the French Catholic Queen Henrietta Maria had ascended the English throne in 1625. By the 1630s it was safer for English travelers to venture into Catholic Rome, and by the 1640s, English Protestants were numbering among the VEC's audience members. The college transitioned more fully into an educational center for English Catholic laity and a travel destination for Englishmen irrespective of their religious faiths. The author John Milton famously visited the college in 1638. The scientist, writer, and colonial administrator John

---

[37] See Dixon, "Music in the Venerable English College in the Early Baroque" and Murata, "*Dal ridicolo al diletto signorile*," "Opera as Spectacle, Opera as Drama," and *Operas for the Papal Court 1631–1668*.

[38] For more detailed explanations of this history, see Jakovac, "Performance Culture at the English College in Rome, *c.* 1579–1660" and my and Maurice Whitehead's "A Stuart Musician's Conversion to Catholicism."

Evelyn wrote that he saw an "Italian comedy" acted at the College in 1644 and then attended "an English play" there in 1645.[39]

My survey of musical dramas at the college compiles surviving indications of theatrical music making along with references to music and sound in VEC play scripts. This material, on a most basic level, tells us that the college was a high-profile site of transcultural musical exchange. It could also help to solve the enduring mystery of what the college music library contained before it was destroyed in the suppression of the society and occupation of Rome by Napoleonic troops. According to VEC dramatic sources, vocal music attributed to English composers was incorporated into at least five seventeenth-century productions at the college. The Latin-language plays, staged before international audiences, employed Italian and French vocal music alongside Italianate English madrigal and ballett repertoires, most or all of it sung in Latin, to dramatize martyrdom. Two later, secular, English-language plays included additional English repertoires, some of it Italianate and apparently all sung in English. The music in these productions seems to have been well known in Britain and might have been chosen with visiting English patrons in mind. Taken together, these performances constitute an extremely rare, if not the only known, case of identifiable English musical repertoires heard by audiences in seventeenth-century Italy. My labeling of certain pieces of music as "English" is not an argument for their distinctive "Englishness" in musical style, but rather a recognition that those pieces were initially published in England by composers who would have identified as Englishmen. What matters here is the movement of this music across the Channel, not whether this music can be described as distinctively English in sound. A large amount of other VEC theatrical music is thought to have originated outside of Britain.

English College students took regular singing lessons, and the college archive theatre records list all manner of musical instruments, including lutes, harps, organs, harpsichords, pipes, drums, bells, and horns.[40] Instrument choices for VEC productions reflect other Roman practices of the time, such as in operas performed at the papal court from the 1630s.[41] The wide variety of instruments played at the VEC is a strong example of transcultural musical activity at the college. On the one hand, theorbos were likely played in VEC dramas, as multiple English lodgers at the VEC purchased theorbos and took theorbo

---

[39] Gossett, "Drama in the English College, Rome, 1591–1660"; Williams, *The Venerable English College Rome,* 42–4.

[40] See Gossett, "Drama in the English College, Rome, 1591–1660," 76–80; Jakovac, "Performance Culture at the English College in Rome, *c.* 1579–1660"; and my and Maurice Whitehead's "A Stuart Musician's Conversion to Catholicism."

[41] See Hammond, *Music & Spectacle in Baroque Rome*, 183–254, and Murata, *Operas for the Papal Court*, 221–389.

lessons; the theorbo was a markedly Italianate musical instrument in Britain, associated with progressive musical genres such as the declamatory continuo song. The English architect and stage designer Inigo Jones is said to have imported the first theorbo to England in 1605. When the instrument arrived at Dover, it was purportedly suspected to be a sinister "Popish" device brought to harm the king. It would take some time for the theorbo to become popular in England, though it had been played throughout Italy since the late sixteenth century.[42] The English College in Rome was no doubt a vector for the instrument's introduction into British musical culture. Multiple lodgers are known to have taken theorbo lessons with Italian and other foreign teachers. One such instructor was likely the famed Austrian–Italian multi-instrumentalist and composer Giovanni Girolamo Kapsperger (c. 1580–1651).[43] To take two examples from personal college account books, between 1626 and 1627, a John Salisbury paid "for lute strings," "for a thorbo mended," and multiple times "for my theorbo maister." In 1630 the future Jesuit missionary Thomas Carvell (Carwell) *vere* Thorold bought "a lute theorbo," strings, and lessons with "my lute master."[44]

On the other hand, the college housed its own viol consort as well; the English viol ensemble tradition of amateur student playing was relatively rare elsewhere in Rome at the time and helped the college stand out from other similar Roman institutions. Viol playing in England remained prevalent much longer than on the Continent.[45] A register of instruments leased by the VEC in the 1630s refers to the college music room as the "room of viols."[46] The English College at Saint-Omer in the Spanish Netherlands, more commonly known in the anglophone world as St. Omer's College, which had its own rich dramatic tradition, maintained both whole and broken student viol consorts. English seminarians typically studied at St. Omer's before arriving in Rome, first receiving much of their musical training at the college in Artois. By the mid-seventeenth century, the VEC itself had garnered a reputation as a venue for exceptional viol performance in Italy.[47] Viol strings

---

[42] See M. Spring, *The Lute in Britain: A History of the Instrument and its Music* (Oxford: Oxford University Press, 2001), 368–99.

[43] See Jakovac, "Performance Culture at the English College in Rome, c. 1579–1660."

[44] "Giovanni Salisbari." Archivum Venerabilis Collegii Anglorum de Urbe (henceforth cited as AVCAU) Liber 309, ff. 24v–25v, 112r. See Jakovac, "Performance Culture at the English College in Rome, *c*. 1579–1660."

[45] For English viols on the Continent, see P. X. del Amo Iribarren, "Anthony Poole (c.1629–1692), the Viol and Exiled English Catholics," unpublished Ph.D. diss., University of Leeds, (2011).

[46] "… camera delle viole." Gossett, "Drama in the English College, Rome, 1591–1660," 79.

[47] del Amo Iribarren, "Anthony Poole (c.1629–1692), the Viol and Exiled English Catholics," 10–20, and W. H. McCabe, "Music and Dance on a 17th-Century College Stage," *The Musical Quarterly* 24, no. 3 (1938): 313–22. For music at St Omers see also P. Leech and M. Whitehead, "'Clamores omnino atque admirationes excitant': New Light on Music and Musicians at St Omers English Jesuit College, 1658–1714," *Tijdschrift van de Koninklijke Vereniging voor Nederlandse Muziekgeschiedenis* 66, no. 1 (2016): 123–48, and "'In Paradise and among

make numerous appearances in personal VEC account books. Instrument strings were an in-demand Italian and especially Roman artistic export throughout Europe.[48] In 1614, for instance, a certain "Mr Boswell" made payments for "viall stringes," and later, in 1632, a "Guglielmo Rolando" purchased his own "violo stringes."[49] This was probably the student William Bretton, alias William Roland, who had studied first at St. Omer's.[50] Butler bought "a boxe of viol strings of all sorts" in 1648.[51] Simons also paid for viol strings in 1652, as well as for "Musicke bookes to send into England" and various manuscript transcriptions of unspecified songs, motets, Masses, and psalms.[52]

Within the narratives of extant college plays, this transcultural musicking virtually always tells a tale of pious "songbirds" battling sacrilegious "screech-owls." A dominant theme running through VEC plays is a dichotomy between serious, heartrending, and celestial Catholic (or Catholic-coded Eastern Orthodox) music and the frivolous, debauched, hellish noisemaking of heretics. Virtuous martyrs and their sympathizers are granted access to musical divinity, while music associated with dramatic villains is pathologized, sexualized, exoticized, racialized, or brutishly militarized. Where musicking falls on either side of this divide is not necessarily determined by a neat differentiation between national repertoires or styles. Rather, this characterological distinction is drawn through timbre, genre, instrumentation, performance practice, and narrative context. Students of the Jesuits were trained to become spiritual soldiers for the Counter-Reformation Church, primed for ideological combat against infidels and idolators.[53] Musical drama at the VEC, however, portrays its protagonists as noble, civilized warriors in contrast to barbaric adversaries, casting Catholic and Catholic-coded characters in a sympathetic light as victimized underdogs.

As Underwood has revealed, VEC sermons from this period, which were similarly given before international congregations in Rome, gendered England as an unnatural (step)mother plagued with the monstrous madness

---

Angels': Music and Musicians at St Omers English Jesuit College, 1593–1721," *Tijdschrift van de Koninklijke Vereniging voor Nederlandse Muziekgeschiedenis* 61, no. 1 (2011): 57–82.

[48] See P. Barbieri, "The Roman Gut String-Makers 1550–1950," *Studi musicali* 35, no. 1 (2006): 3–127.

[49] AVCAU Liber 262, f. 104v, and Liber 309, f. 155r.

[50] A. Kenny (ed.), *The Responsa Scholarum of the English College, Rome*, Vol. 2 (Newport: The Catholic Record Society, 1963), 428–9.

[51] AVCAU Liber 314, f. 26v. For Butler at the VEC, see my and Maurice Whitehead's "A Stuart Musician's Conversion to Catholicism."

[52] AVCAU Liber 314, f. 75v.

[53] For a recent study, see C. Archibald, "Actors, Soldiers, and Jesuits in Post-Reformation England: Joseph Simons' 1648 Oration on Robert Persons and the Mission to England," *The Seventeenth Century* 40, no. 2 (2025): 249–95.

of Protestantism, a condition painted as an aberration from her true Catholic nature. Within England's metaphorical family triangle, the pope was positioned as father and English priests as her physician-sons striving to cure her condition.[54] Constructions of a genteel, rational Catholic masculinity battling a feminized oppositional force can be found in many other Jesuit plays performed far beyond the Anglo-Italian context. In a case study on musical theatre at the Colegio Máximo de San Pedro y San Pablo in Mexico City, for example, Stephanie Kirk has demonstrated that Jesuit dramatizations of Catholic martyrdom in the colonies of New Spain espoused a proscriptive image of heroic masculinity based on erudition, self-restraint, and self-sacrifice, leaving the martyr's adversaries to fill the deleterious role of uncivilized Others.[55]

Musically, these tensions played out on the VEC stage as a vicious conflict between heavenly harmony and sonic vulgarity. In the seventeenth century, it was widely thought that musical dissonance, disorder, and excess were linked to a moral deficiency caused by a musical practitioner's or listener's own internal humoral imbalance; in other words, ugly or self-indulgent music making was a symptom of ill physio-psychological health. Early modern drama was saturated with Neoplatonic symbolism that bluntly contrasted divine concinnity with discordant noise. Harsh sounds both on and off-stage, considered a demented corruption of *musica mundana*, the harmony of the spheres, was associated with mental disorder, moral decay, physio-spiritual misalignment, and estrangement from God.[56] VEC representations of English martyrs and their analogues would have presented to the college's audiences an image of England as a fundamentally Catholic country possessed by the infernal madness of the Protestant faith. This study shows how, according to such messaging, the Reformation was represented as a national affliction, while the graceful musicking of English recusants remained a connecting thread between their "fairest isle" and the salubrious cultural values of Catholic Europe.

These ideas about music and sound also pervaded the Jesuit theatre as doctrinal themes. One play performed in 1583 at the Jesuit College in Fulda, *Dialogus Musicae*, parodied Heinrich Cornelius Agrippa von Nettesheim's

---

[54] Underwood, "Representing England in Rome," 19–23.
[55] Kirk, "Relics, Jesuit Masculinity, and the Performance of Martyrdom in *Triumpho de los Sanctos*."
[56] See L. P. Austern, *Both from the Ears and Mind: Thinking about Music in Early Modern England* (Chicago: University of Chicago Press, 2020), 217–68; P. Gouk, "Music and Spirit in Early Modern Thought," in E. Carrera (ed.), *Emotions and Health, 1200–1700* (Leiden: Brill, 2013), 221–39; B. Varwig, *Music in the Flesh: An Early Modern Musical Physiology* (Chicago: University of Chicago Press, 2023), 209–30; and A. E. Winkler, *O Let Us Howle Some Heavy Note: Music for Witches, the Melancholic, and the Mad on the Seventeenth-Century English Stage* (Bloomington: Indiana University Press, 2006).

(1486–1535) writings on the virtues of different church musics: In it, a nightingale and cuckoo agree that animals that bark, grunt, moo, and whinny are unfit judges for their cherubic birdsong competition.[57] Roman Jesuit dramas, for example Agostino Agazzari's 1606 *dramma pastorale Eumelio* at the Seminario Romano, condemned dance and other profane, lascivious forms of musicking as morally inferior to more pure-hearted musical devotions to God.[58] The VEC theatre also inherited many sonic characterological signifiers from the English secular stage as well as Italian *commedia dell'arte*, madrigal comedy, and *intermedio* traditions. The Counter-Reformation church had a conflictual relationship with sensuous and coarse *commedia* entertainments, denouncing them as obscene while still appropriating them for religious instruction.[59] The English theatre similarly approached musical excess and disharmony with ambivalence, damning these tendencies as perverse while, paradoxically, titillating listeners by sounding them out on-stage.[60]

The VEC's Roman and English spectator-auditors alike would have assumed that decadent or disagreeable sounds were the purview of rogues, monsters, demons, occultists, mad kings, and other sinister sorts. These "noisy" characters inhabit what was also a harmful racialized sonic profile of non-Christian, non-European cultures.[61] To take one example elaborated below, VEC dramas associate the *moresca* and other militaristic dances with villains. Many Jesuit colleges on the Continent specialized in choreographed martial dances such as the pyrrhic and *moresca*, as they exemplified the society's militaristic pedagogy designed to discipline seminarians into soldiers for the Church.[62] These dance forms, however, also served a pointed dramatic purpose. In both English and Italian theatre, trumpets, drums, fifes, and other martial instruments represented a distinctly unmusical, barbarous sound. In courtly spectacle across Europe, their blaring and rumbling effects

---

[57] F. Körndle, "Between Stage and Divine Service: Jesuits and Theatrical Music," in P. Vendrix (ed.), *Music and the Renaissance: Renaissance, Reformation and Counter-Reformation* (London: Routledge, 2011), 486–89.

[58] Lyon, "Magis corde quam organo."

[59] B. Majorana, "Commedia dell'Arte and the Church," in C. B. Balme, P. Vescovo, and D. Vianello (eds.), *Commedia dell'Arte in Context* (Cambridge: Cambridge University Press, 2018), 133–48.

[60] Winkler, *O Let Us Howle Some Heavy Note*.

[61] For some of these characterizations in other contexts, see Lamothe, "The Theater of Piety," 228–92; Varwig, *Music in the Flesh*, 225–30; E. Wilbourne, "Music, Race, Representation: Three Scenes of Performance at the Medici Court (1608–16)," *Il saggiatore musicale* 27, no. 1 (2020): 5–168; Winkler, *O Let Us Howle Some Heavy Note*; J. L. Wood, *Sounding Otherness in Early Modern Drama and Travel: Uncanny Vibrations in the English Archive* (Cham: Palgrave Macmillan, 2019); and L. J. Wright, *Sound Effects: Hearing the Early Modern Stage* (Manchester: Manchester University Press, 2023).

[62] K. van Orden, *Music, Discipline, and Arms in Early Modern France* (Chicago: University of Chicago Press, 2005), 187–234.

typically evoked ferocious madness and the warlike clamor associated with heathen, foreign Otherness, such as Ottoman Janissary music. These wind and percussive cavalry instruments were racially marked in Italy, as enslaved Black laborers were frequently trained to play them.[63]

In Italian theatre, musical sophistication belonged primarily to serious *innamorati* archetypes, more socially elevated characters who expressed their emotions and showcased their musical skill by singing madrigals and laments. The singing of melancholic music, however, also ran the risk of plunging a drama's *innamorati* into madness.[64] In England, where women rarely sang on public stages, laments carried connotations of effeminacy and erotomania. As was the case in Jesuit theatre, musicking women and effeminate music were viewed with suspicion as treacherous pathways to inflamed passions and immoral behavior. Sounds made by dangerous women on the English stage, such as incantations by witches, were usually coded as Catholic.[65] VEC plays flip this characterization upside down, instead burdening Protestant and other heretical antagonists with sonic demonstrations of madness, lewdness, and beastliness. Conversely, martyrs are ensconced within moving musical elegies and sacred musical splendor while themselves steering clear of musical melancholia. In this respect, VEC dramas followed an English theatrical convention that Amanda Eubanks Winkler has termed "ventriloquized lament." The distress of male protagonists was oftentimes expressed indirectly through another singing character, typically a servant or younger boy, so as to shield more upstanding male characters from musical descent into madness and a resulting loss of masculine rationality.[66] In VEC dramas, martyrs generally do not sing. So goes the old adage, "Jesuita non cantat" ("a Jesuit does not sing"). Just as the society decried overuse of music in the liturgy while ironically becoming one of the most musically influential

---

[63] E. Rosand, *Opera in Seventeenth-Century Venice: The Creation of a Genre* (Berkeley: University of California Press, 1991), 346–60; Wilbourne, "Music, Race, Representation," 31, *Seventeenth-Century Opera and the Sound of the Commedia dell'Arte* (Chicago: University of Chicago Press, 2016), 19–27, and *Voice, Slavery, and Race in Seventeenth-Century Florence* (Oxford: Oxford University Press, 2023); Wood, *Sounding Otherness in Early Modern Drama and Travel*; Wright, *Sound Effects*.

[64] See A. E. MacNeil, "Celestial Sirens of the Commedia dell'Arte Stage," in J. Chaffee and O. Crick (eds.), *The Routledge Companion to the Commedia dell'Arte* (London: Routledge, 2015), 246–54, and "Commedia dell'Arte in Opera and Music 1550–1750," in Balme, Vescovo, and Vianello (eds.), *Commedia dell'Arte in Context*, 167–76; M. Murata, "The Recitative Soliloquy," *Journal of the American Musicological Society* 32, no. 1 (1979): 45–73; Rosand, *Opera in Seventeenth-Century Venice*, 361–96, and "The Descending Tetrachord: An Emblem of Lament," *The Musical Quarterly* 65, no. 3 (1979): 346–59; and Wilbourne, *Seventeenth-Century Opera and the Sound of the Commedia dell'Arte*.

[65] Winkler, *O Let Us Howle Some Heavy Note*.

[66] Winkler, *O Let Us Howle Some Heavy Note*, 134–9.

institutions in early modern Europe, on-stage, the martyr remains silent while still leaving a lush musical treat in his wake.[67]

In this research, I did not seek to write a comprehensive reception history of musical theatre at the college, but I have gathered some fragmentary evidence attesting to an enthusiastic reception of English Jesuit drama in mainland Europe. One martyr play presented at the English College of Saint Alban in Valladolid, for example, was said to have moved city magnates to pity and tears. Similarly, a Passion play acted at St. Omer's purportedly stirred feelings of intense religious devotion in audience members.[68] VEC productions in particular were consistently well attended and received mention more than once in the *avvisi di Roma*, or, newsletters reporting on contemporary political and cultural happenings across the city.[69] One *avviso* on *Zeno* describes the production's mock battle as "a wonder to behold."[70] Carleton's disapproving dispatches about *Captiva* provide a rare English Protestant perspective on musical drama at the VEC, and another description of the same play by the Venetian spy Federico Gotardi – evidently one of Carleton's informants – gives a more mixed review, praising the acting but also adding that the play had been too long and dull.[71] Two years later, Gotardi exclaimed that an English College production of *Campianus*, a play about the martyrdom of the English Jesuit Edmund Campion (1540–81), had, out of all other tragedies staged in Rome that year, "been the pride, and in truth it was most exquisite, as much for the nobility of the work as for the excellence of the actors." He recalled that the students' Latin pronunciation had sounded so Roman

> that many of them seemed to have been born not in England, but in Lazio: and then their music, dances, and combat scenes are unsurpassed in these regions, and I know that some, just seeing these youths appear onstage, striking and modest in angel costumes, could not stop themselves from weeping ... [I]n Rome there is no foreign nation more beloved than that of the English for the great conformity it has with Italian civility.[72]

---

[67] See A. Cichy, "Scheming Jesuits and Sound Doctrine?: The Influence of the Jesuits on English Catholic Music at Home and Abroad, c.1580–1640" in J. E. Kelly and H. Thomas (eds.), *Jesuit Intellectual and Physical Exchange between England and Mainland Europe, c. 1580–1789: "The World is Our House?"* (Leiden: Brill, 2019), 133–51.

[68] Murphy, "Music and Post-Reformation English Catholics," 74–6.

[69] Gossett, "Drama in the English College, Rome, 1591–1660," 60; Murata, "*Dal ridicolo al diletto signorile*," 271.

[70] *Avviso di Roma* on *Zeno* in Jakovac, "Performance Culture at the English College in Rome, c. 1579–1660."

[71] See Federico Gotardi to Alvise Boncasio, February 8, 15, and 22, 1614, State Papers 85/4, ff. 99r–103v, TNA.

[72] "... portato il vanto, et in vero è stata cosa isguisitiss:[a], si per la nobiltà del componimento, come per l'eccellenza dè recitanti ... " " ... che molti di loro parevano nati non in Inghilterra, ma nel Latio: le suoni poi, li balli, et combatimenti della loro scena non hanno piu in questi paesi, et sò

Gotardi's words acutely illustrate how successfully the VEC garnered attention and affection for England in Italy by assimilating into Roman theatrical culture. Finally, it is known that, at the insistence of the cardinals, the college staged the tragedy *S. Thomas Cantuariensis* five times in 1613, and it was met with great applause by all.[73] As we shall see, this is one of few productions for which musical notation survives.

3 *Thomas Morus*, 1612

The earliest identifiable piece of music in an English College play appears in *Thomas Morus*, an anonymously authored Latin drama about the martyrdom of the English Catholic politician and humanist Thomas More (1478–1535) during the Henrician Reformation. The play was performed at the college three times in February 1612 and survives only in two VEC manuscripts. College theatre records show that a violinist normally employed by Cardinal Giovanni Battista Deti was hired for the occasion.[74] In one script from VEC manuscript Liber 321, when More's deceased body is solemnly carried forward in the final scene of the drama, music begins to play ("Music is heard"; Figure 1) and More's son John declares that "the sound of More welcomes the heavenly feast." The music then starts up once again and John More wonders aloud if the earth is beginning to harmonize with his lament. Perhaps, he muses, the musical modes and proportions might bring some structure to the comparatively unmeasured chaos of his tears. This alludes to contemporary assumptions about the healing capacity of terrestrial music making to align *musica humana*, or the internal systems of the human body, with the harmony of the spheres.[75] As the martyred Thomas More ascends to celestial sainthood, making music allows his grieving son to also partake in his "heavenly feast." These Neoplatonic associations would have been strengthened if, as it seems, the source of the play's music was concealed. In early modern theatre and ceremonial, hidden music was often deployed to

---

che alcuni col solo vedere questi giovani apparire in scena, vistosi et modesti in guisa d'angeli, non si potevano contenere dal lagrime ... [I]n Roma non ce sia natione forestiera piu amata che [quella] Inglese per la gran conformità che hà nella civilità con l'Italiano ... " Gotardi to Cornelio Celso, February 13, 1616, State Papers 85/5, f. 7r, TNA. Jakovac has recently discovered this play's title and *argomento*. See Jakovac, "Performance Culture at the English College in Rome, *c*. 1579–1660."

[73] Gossett, "Drama in the English College, Rome, 1591–1660," 88. See also Jakovac, "Performance Culture at the English College in Rome, *c*. 1579–1660."

[74] AVCAU Liber 321 contains three copies of the text and there is also a fragment in AVCAU Scrittura 33/5. See Jakovac, "Performance Culture at the English College in Rome, *c*. 1579–1660"; D. Sutton (ed.), "The Anonymous Tragedy *Thomas Morus* (1612)," *The Philological Museum* (updated May 24, 2005), https://philological.cal.bham.ac.uk/more/; and Wiggins and Richardson, "1670. *Thomas Morus*" in *British Drama 1533–1642*, Vol. 6.

[75] "Caeleste festis excipit Morum sonus," "Auditur musica," *Thomas Morus*, Act V, Scene 5, ACVAU Liber 321, f. 46r.

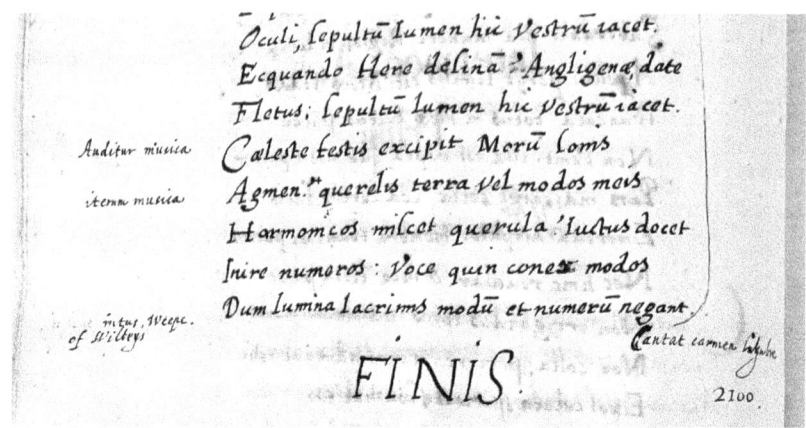

Figure 1 Music at the end of *Thomas Morus* (1612), Act V, Scene 5. Archivum Venerabilis Collegii Anglorum de Urbe (AVCAU) Liber 321, f. 46r, Image copyright© the Venerable English College, Rome: reproduced with permission

inspire awe in spectator-auditors and so represent the patrons who produced such sounds as divinely anointed masters of natural magic.[76]

At the end of John More's final monologue, the script's marginalia indicate that he proceeds to "sing a mournful song" (Figure 1). Written in the left-hand margin directly across from that is the phrase, "From within they play Weepe ... of Wilbey's." The text for "they play" ("Ludunt") is nearly faded but legible. There appears to be further deleted, indecipherable text between "Weepe" and "of Wilbey's." This text, perhaps erased on purpose, could possibly say "weepe" once more or describe the type of piece performed. The annotation could refer to either of two madrigals by the English composer John Wilbye (1574–1638): the three-voice "Weepe O Mine Eies" from his *First Set of English Madrigals to 3. 4. 5. And 6. Voices*, printed in London in 1598, or the five-part "Weepe, Mine Eyes" from Wilbye's *Second Set of Madrigales to 3. 4. 5. and 6. Parts*, printed in London in 1609.[77] The English text of the first madrigal (written below) would have been well suited to the drama's narrative context, but Wilbye's printed

---

[76] See e.g. A. Spohr, "Concealed Music in Early Modern Diplomatic Ceremonial," in R. Ahrendt, M. Ferraguto, and D. Mahiet (eds.), *Music and Diplomacy from the Early Modern Era to the Present* (New York: Palgrave Macmillan, 2014), 19–43; and N. Treadwell, *Music and Wonder at the Medici Court: The 1589 Interludes for* La Pellegrina (Bloomington: Indiana University Press, 2008), and "Music of the Gods: Solo Song and *effetti meravigliosi* in the Interludes for *La pellegrina*," *Current Musicology* 83 (2007): 33–84.

[77] "Cantat carmen lulgubre," "Ludunt intus Weepe ... of Wilbey's." *Thomas Morus*, Act V, Scene 5, AVCAU Liber 321, f. 46r. J. Wilbye, *The First Set of English Madrigals to 3. 4. 5. And 6. Voices* (London: Printed by T. Este, 1598), no. 4, and *The Second Set of Madrigales to 3. 4. 5. and 6. Parts* (London: Printed by T. Este for J. Browne, 1609), no. 23.

edition of the latter madrigal sets an English text about the Greco-Roman tale of Hero and Leander, which hardly seems appropriate for the play's subject matter. It is possible that John More sang a different unnamed melody at the end and that a piece by Wilbye was only performed by offstage instruments before the character's song. If John More's lament was indeed set to either madrigal tune, however, its text might have been altered, most likely as a Latin contrafactum.

> Weepe O mine eies & cease not:
> Your spring tides out alas,
> Me thinks increase not.
>
> O when begin you,
> To swell so high,
> That I may drowne me in you?[78]

Well into the seventeenth century, alongside the emergence of recitational Italian monody, the polyphonic madrigal remained one of the most popular forms of secular music in Rome. Seicento Italian singers continued to perform madrigals as solo songs with somewhat improvised instrumental accompaniment.[79] The Italian madrigal, both on and off-stage, was also an important laboratory for early musical experimentation with the *stile moderno*.[80] Wilbye and his English contemporaries famously embraced the Italian madrigal as a fashionable musical model across the Channel, which resulted in an abundance of English madrigal composition in the decades leading up to the VEC's performance of *Thomas Morus*. Notably, Philips and Dering, who had both been musicians-in-residence at the VEC, were two such champions of English madrigal repertoires. Wilbye, however, was, as much as can be gleaned from the historical record, a Protestant who never visited the college.[81]

Stylistically, either madrigal by Wilbye would have been an appropriate fit for the Roman theatre. Though generally somber in character, "Weepe, Mine Eyes" contains dramatic contrasts between sustained passages of languid suspensions passed between voices and more declamatory, homophonic outbursts of grief, a juxtaposition that characterized the progressive Italian *seconda pratica*. Like the work of well-known Italian madrigalists such as Luca Marenzio (c. 1553–99) and Claudio Monteverdi (1567–1643), "Weepe, Mine Eyes" also employs affective musical devices such as proto-tonal, large-scale major–minor inflection, and sequential multi-voice transposition on repeated phrases of text. Even so, as

---

[78] Wilbye, *First Set of English Madrigals to 3. 4. 5. And 6. Voices*, no. 4.
[79] D. V. Filippi, "*Roma Sonora*: An Atlas of Roman Sounds and Musics," in Jones, Wisch, and Ditchfield, (eds.), *A Companion to Early Modern Rome, 1492–1692*, 270–1.
[80] See, for example, E. Rosand, "Monteverdi's Mimetic Art: *L'Incoronazione di Poppea*," *Cambridge Opera Journal* 1, no. 2 (1989): 113–37.
[81] See D. Brown, "Wilbye [Willoughbye], John" in *Grove Music Online*, *Oxford Music Online* (2001), https://doi.org/10.1093/gmo/9781561592630.article.30302.

Figure 2 Excerpt from John Wilbye, "Weepe, Mine Eyes," *The Second Set of Madrigales to 3. 4. 5. and 6. Parts*. London: Printed by Thomas Este for John Browne, 1609

scholars such as Kian-Seng Teo have noted about Wilbye's madrigals, the piece is markedly less chromatic than many of its Italian counterparts.[82]

To take one passage from "Weepe, Mine Eyes" that showcases Monteverdian stylistic choices (Figure 2), the second part of the madrigal begins with the predominantly homophonic declamation "Aye me, ah, cruell Fortune, Aye me," reminiscent of a recitative in its imitation of speech rhythms. Also following Italian models, the second iteration of "Aye me" (Figure 2, m. 4) sounds a dissonant suspension in the lower two voices over a flat sixth in the bass. The Phrygian Inflection is a recurring expressive device in the Italian madrigal repertoire, especially in text settings about weeping and lament.[83]

By contrast, "Weepe O Mine Eies" does not embrace a progressive Italianate style, although Wilbye's first book of madrigals does take after Marenzio's early work.[84] Both madrigals begin with descending *lachrimae* motives (Figures 3 and 4), which are a distinctive trait of the English madrigal and viol repertoire, notably in the compositions of Morley and Philips.[85] In "Weepe, Mine Eyes,"

---

[82] For Wilbye and his Italian models, see K. Teo, "John Wilbye's Second Set of Madrigals (1609) and the Influence of Marenzio and Monteverdi," *Studies in Music* 20 (1986): 1–11.

[83] See M. Medić, "From Pain to Pleasure: The Troping of Elegy in the Renaissance Italian Madrigal," *Muzikologija* 1, no. 22 (2017): 151–75.

[84] Teo, "John Wilbye's Second Set of Madrigals (1609) and the Influence of Marenzio and Monteverdi."

[85] For an extensive analysis of the *lachrimae* motive in Wilbye and other early modern English music, see J. Bryan, "'*Full of Art*, and *Profundity*': The Five-Part Consort Pavan as a Medium for Sophisticated Musical Expression and Compositional Cross-Reference in Late Renaissance

Figure 3 *Lachrimae* opening of Wilbye, "Weepe O Mine Eies," *The First Set of English Madrigals to 3. 4. 5. And 6. Voices*. London: Printed by Thomas Este, 1598

all voices then repeat this opening *lachrimae* phrase in a transposition up a fourth from D into G, a practice indicative of newer Italian influences.

If either madrigal is indeed the piece that John More sang, which seems most plausible given the layout of the script's marginalia, his voice might have been joined by a solo instrument or an instrumental consort playing the lower parts notated in Wilbye's earlier printed editions, or perhaps by a sparser basso continuo line.[86] The plural form of "Ludunt" implies that multiple musicians had been playing the offstage music before John More began to sing. They might have all continued to accompany his song. If he performed "Weepe, Mine Eyes" as a solo vocal piece, it could have sounded something like the highly ornamented Italianate version for solo voice and continuo surviving in British Library Egerton Manuscript 2971. Like *Thomas Morus*, this manuscript songbook dates from the second decade of the seventeenth century. Its earliest owner was a certain Robert Downes. This might have been the recusant Norfolk Catholic by the same name, imprisoned for harboring priests in his home and thought to be the brother of the priest and English College alumnus Edmund

---

England" in D. J. Smith and R. Taylor (eds.), *Networks of Music and Culture in the Late Sixteenth and Early Seventeenth Centuries* (London: Routledge, 2013), 185–201.

[86] Gossett, "Drama in the English College, Rome, 1591–1660," 76–80.

Figure 4 *Lachrimae* opening of Wilbye, "Weepe, Mine Eyes"

Downes (born 1575).[87] The manuscript's solo setting of the madrigal is decorated with numerous elaborate Italianate divisions, even doubling the length of the antepenultimate and penultimate notes to make room for further ornaments (Figure 5).[88] In this solo form, Wilbye's madrigal certainly veers into the territory of Seicento Italian monody.

---

[87] H. Foley, *Records of the English Province of the Society of Jesus*, Vol. 7 (London: Burns and Oates, 1882), 208; and M. Reynolds, *Godly Reformers and their Opponents in Early Modern England: Religion in Norwich, c.1560–1643* (Woodbridge: Boydell and Brewer, 2005), 205.

[88] Egerton MS 2971, British Library, London (henceforth GB-Lbl). For this manuscript version, see R. Toft, *With Passionate Voice: Re-Creative Singing in Sixteenth-Century England and Italy* (Oxford: Oxford University Press, 2014), https://doi.org/10.1093/ml/gcv120.

Figure 5 Final measures of Wilbye, "Weepe, Mine Eyes," Egerton Manuscript 2971. British Library, London

The musical affinity of Wilbye's compositions with the work of Italian madrigalists and the possible accompaniment of his pieces on Italianate continuo instruments such as the theorbo would have probably rendered John More's song legible to the VEC's audiences as a poignant expression of sorrow. A contrafactum of either piece in Latin, a language shared by English seminarians and their ecclesiastical Roman listeners, would have enabled the VEC to communicate More's story across cultures and elicit foreign sympathy for anti-Catholic religious persecution in England. "Weepe, Mine Eyes" in particular, though composed in a progressive Italianate musical idiom, does also possess somewhat unique characteristics associated with more English musical repertoires, especially its use of the opening *lachrimae* motive. To add another dimension of cultural complexity, the piece's possible performance by a student viol consort could have intrigued foreign listeners by showcasing the English viol ensemble tradition. Instrumentation and ornamentation aside, the piece could have been sung in Latin and its musical style might have sounded Italianate, and yet, it was attached to an English character and had been published abroad by an Englishman only three years prior. It is doubtful that the show's foreign spectator-auditors had heard either madrigal before. The theatrical presentation of these pieces alone would have likely been a novelty in Rome.[89]

Most kinsmen of martyrs do not sing in English College dramas, but *Thomas Morus* is a rare example of ventriloquized lament in which the martyr's son, John More, is selected as the surrogate musician to grieve in song. Nevertheless, John More does fit the typical dramatic profile of a younger male character deployed to shoulder the responsibility of musical lamentation, in this case for his slain father. And it is still a righteous Catholic character who sings an affecting dirge. No Protestant in *Thomas Morus* utters anything close to this harmonious music. In stark relief against this sweet lament that John More warbles for his martyred father, King Henry VIII and his court indulge in raucous musical delights with

---

[89] For English viols on the Continent, see del Amo Iribarren, "Anthony Poole (c.1629–1692), the Viol and Exiled English Catholics."

violent overtones; Henry's courtiers perform a militaristic all-male ensemble dance before the king in Act II, Scene 3, while a chorus exclaims that the king is deceitful and they are living in an evil time.[90] Such choruses in VEC plays might have been sung rather than spoken by groups of students. Based on Jesuit dramatic practices elsewhere, these choruses probably would have been composed in a hymn-like homophonic manner.[91]

Not only does John More express his grief by apparently singing in an Italianate madrigalian style, but, leading up to that point, he also explicitly announces himself to be a singer of Italian music. In one manuscript version of the play, he performs an unnamed Italian song in Latin in Act III, Scene 4, in which he condemns the wickedness of Henry VIII and his court. John More sings that the song had first been sent to his father. No musical notation survives. The only extant indication of the piece's "Italianness" appears in the final lines of the song text itself:

Prudens cupit	*He wants to be called the prudent type*
Genus vocari, perfidum iustè potest:	*But can justly be called treacherous.*
Privata damno publico crescit domus,	*His private household grows by public loss.*
Mercede cuncta librat, exitium lues	*He balances everything with a price, that ruin, that plague,*
Et aura Regni pestibus, auro nefas	*And the air of the Kingdom is pestilent.*
Mercatur, auro vendit impunè fidem	*He buys sin with gold, he sells faith for gold with impunity.*
Corruptus, auro pròdidit Caelum, Deum.	*Corrupted by gold, he betrayed Heaven and God.*
Sed faeminam auro proximum mundo malum	*But the woman, the next evil in the world after gold,*
Praetereo tacitus: regnat Henricus: malis	*I pass by in silence: Henry reigns:*
Subducere satis sit tibi temet, puer.	*Let it be enough for you to hide yourself from evils, boy.*
Dic instrumenti cantibus meis sonus	*Say that the sound of the instrument fits my songs.*
Aptet.[r]: Italum canto quem misit patri	*I sing the Italian one which that friend sent to my father.*
Amicus ille, fallet innocuum melos	*The harmless melody will make us forget those things*
Quae fallit horam plurimos	*Which most people can forget for an hour.*[92]

---

[90] Act II, Scene 3, Sutton (ed.), "The Anonymous Tragedy *Thomas Morus* (1612)."

[91] Gossett, "Drama in the English College, Rome, 1591–1660," 80; Körndle, "Between Stage and Divine Service."

[92] This is not Sutton's translation but rather one made by Michael Ennis, Rebecca Villareal, one of my readers, and myself. John More, Act III, Scene 4, *Thomas Morus,* Liber 321, f. 25r.

John More's words pick up the same rhetoric that Underwood has highlighted in VEC sermons, as his song describes the English Reformation as a plague and Henry VIII as corrupted by worldly riches and the feminine wiles of Anne Boleyn. John More's self-proclaimed singing of Italian music to accompany this criticism of the Tudor court, presumably followed by an Italianate madrigal by Wilbye as an elegy for the martyred Thomas More, draws associations between English adoption of Italian musical influences and England's sixteenth-century connections to papal Rome. This may or may not have registered with the VEC's audiences, but the play's English historical subject matter, musical offerings, and maybe even instrumentation choices might have made a unique contribution to the Roman theatre and helped the VEC to stand out as an English cultural institution.

4 *Minutum*, 1613

The next surviving pieces of VEC theatre music were apparently sung just one year later in *Minutum*, a Latin *intermedio* of unknown authorship inserted between the acts of *S. Thomas Cantuariensis*, presented at the college in 1613 and again in 1617. *Minutum* was revived at least once more in a 1634 VEC production of *Zeno*.[93] *Minutum*, preserved only in a Liber 321 copy of *S. Thomas Cantuariensis*, is a series of dialogues between months of the year as they compete for the attention of the Greco-Roman god Saturn. October, November, and December are quarrelsome and violent, as they constitute the season in which the twelfth-century Archbishop of Canterbury, Thomas Becket, was martyred. April, May, and June, however, are more distant from the tragedy; they dance and play a lighthearted musical game of deciding whether to give Saturn the gift of tearful showers or cheerful maying. April votes for rain, May desires revelry, and June breaks the tie to make May the winner.[94] Such whimsical comic plots were typical of *intermedi* in multiple Roman Jesuit colleges. Liber 321 contains melodic notation for two songs in Act II (Figures 6–12), the latter of which sets a three-verse Latin text, "Iam lenis spirat aura," to the tune of Thomas Morley's "Now is the Month of Maying," published in his 1595 *First Booke of Balletts to Five Voyces* and originally based on an earlier sixteenth-century Italian *balletto* by Orazio Vecchi (1550–1605), "So ben mi c'ha bon tempo."[95] Vecchi's madrigal and other light repertoires were a regular feature of the Italian comic theatre.[96]

---

[93] D. Sutton (ed.), "The Intermedium *Minutum* (1613)," *The Philological Museum* (updated August 2, 2006), https://philological.cal.bham.ac.uk/minutum?/, and Wiggins and Richardson, "1696. *Sanctus Thomas Cantuariensis*" and "1697. *Minutum*" in *British Drama 1533–1642*, Vol. 6.

[94] Sutton (ed.), "The Intermedium *Minutum* (1613)," and Wiggins and Richardson, "1696. *Sanctus Thomas Cantuariensis*" and "1697. *Minutum*."

[95] Act II, *Minutum*, Liber 321, ff. 102r–121r; T. Morley, *The First Booke of Balletts to Five Voyces*. (London: T. Este, 1595), no. 3.

[96] Wilbourne, *Seventeenth-Century Opera and the Sound of the Commedia dell'Arte*, 38–42.

May is the first character to strike up the music performed in Act II. He enters singing the nonsense syllables "La, la, la, la, &c." and then exclaims, "Come hither, you murmuring nightingales, you deep-sounding crested larks, you blackbirds that whimper among yourselves, you god-greeting herons, you sweet-complaining songbirds, and whatever exists in the feathered choir of forest-dwelling birds, come hither, I say, and join me in caressing the springtime with your little sweet songs."[97]

When birds begin to chirp in response, June expresses instead a preference for birds that would excite his laughter, and so he bursts into the act's first notated song, the through-composed "Nuntie, nuntie" (Figures 6–8). He initially calls to awaken Spring in triple time on the word "Nuntie" before settling into a duple meter to summon his own favorite birds:

Nuntie, nuntie,	O harbinger, harbinger,
O laeti remeantis anni,	The happy returning year,
Vividum terrae renovans colorem,	Bringing back the land's bright color,
Huc ades, huc ades,	Come here, come here,
Fundens roseos odores	Shedding your rosy scents,
Ver rediviuum, ver rediviuum,	Reborn springtime, reborn springtime,
Te melo pictae volucres canoro,	Many-colored birds with their tuneful voice,
Te loquax sylvae resonantis	Of the resonating wood, the garrulous,
Echo, Echo,	Echo, Echo,
Te tuus blandè redeunte	[And], while you return, sweetly,
Maius, Maius,	Your May, your May,
Voce salutat, voce salutat.	Greet you with their voice, greet you with their voice.[98]

June's song goes unanswered. May instructs him, "[W]ith your sighs, June, alas, you give an accompaniment. Rather you should be adapting your voice to the little birds' tunes."[99] In encouraging June's assimilation into an animal's musical language, a cultural accommodation of its own kind, May could refer to the constant intervallic leaps that June's vocal melody makes. June did, after all, appeal directly to "tuneful" songbirds. Nonetheless, long pauses between and sustained notes within musical phrases in "Nuntie" also imply possible missing instrumental parts and suggest that June's melody functioned as one of multiple voices within a polyphonic texture. June's song is followed by May's tune, Morley's "Iam lenis spirat aura." This melody is more stepwise and contains fewer sustained note values, especially at cadences. May also eschews June's

---

[97] May, Act II, Sutton (ed.), "The Intermedium *Minutum* (1613)."

[98] I have slightly edited Sutton's translation. Thanks are due to one of my anonymous readers for assisting with this retranslation. June, Act II, Sutton (ed.), "The Intermedium *Minutum* (1613)."

[99] May, Act II, Sutton (ed.), "The Intermedium *Minutum* (1613)."

English Madrigals on the Jesuit Stage 31

Figure 6 First page of "Nuntie, nuntie," *Minutum* (1613) Act II. AVCAU Liber 321, f. 108r. Image copyright © the Venerable English College, Rome: reproduced with permission

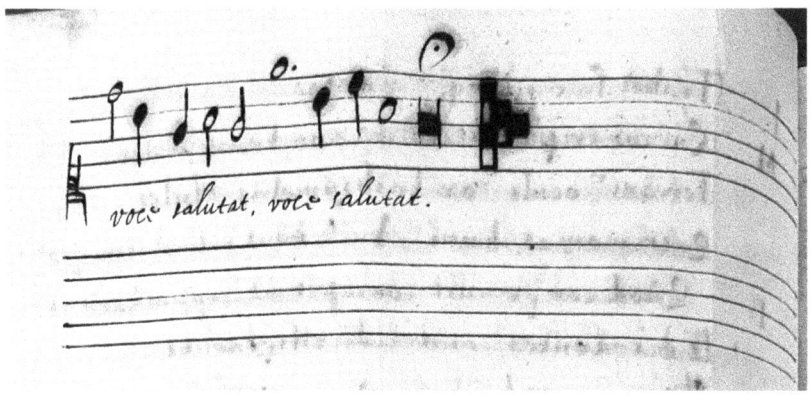

Figure 7 Second page of "Nuntie, nuntie," f. 108v. Image copyright © the Venerable English College, Rome: reproduced with permission

echo effects in favor of more nonsense syllables that appear to mimic the chirruping of birds ("ta na no"). The woods are more partial to this piece, which is accompanied by both birdsong and whistling wind. April and June then pick up the tune in two more musical strophes.

Figure 8 Transcription of "Nuntie, nuntie"

MAY

Iam lenis spirat aura,	*Now the gentle wind blows,*
Et Maium cingit Flora,	*And Flora embraces May*
Ta na no &c.	*Ta na no &c.*
Proles iocosá veris	*Let us playful children of springtime*
Misceamus cantum serijs.	*Mix our song with serious things*
Ta na no &c.	*Ta na no &c.*

APRIL

Stillat Aprilis rores,	*April drips his dews,*
Queis Maio vernant flores,	*Thanks to which flowers in May grow green,*

Ta na no &c.	*Ta na no &c.*
Alternis ergo locis	*Therefore in turns let us*
Misceamus fletum iocis;	*Mix weeping with our sports;*
Ta na no &c.	*Ta na no &c.*

JUNE

At Junius suadet umbras,	*But June urges shades,*
Dum vergit sol ad undas,	*As the sun inclines toward the waves,*
Ta na no &c.	*Ta na no &c.*
Choreas io laetas,	*Let us perform our happy dances*
Ducamus, transit aetas.	*Our age is passing by.*
Ta na no &c.	*Ta na no &c.*[100]

The only melody given is for May (Figures 9 and 11), under which are added two other verses of text for April and June (Figure 10), labeled as "Fitting the words to the above-given notes."[101] The song concludes the scene and ends with a satyr dance, possibly to the same tune; this particular ballett was well suited to dances such as the branle.[102] Satyr dances were a favorite feature of not only Italian *intermedi* but also English masques.[103]

This VEC variant of Morley's melody diverges somewhat from its earlier printed form (Figure 12), for example in the manuscript's first phrase, which jumps up from the D fifth below rather than starting on a G scale degree one (Figure 11). It also lacks a raised accidental on the fourth (Figures 11, m. 3, and 12, m. 3). This same lowered fourth appears in a solo manuscript version of the ballett for soprano and lute in British Library Additional Manuscript 15117, dating from around 1614–16. In this songbook, however, the piece is given a new text, entitled, "The Peacefull Westerne Winde" (Figure 13, poetry by Thomas Campion). The songbook belonged initially to a John Swarland and then to a Hugh Floyd. In Add. MS 15117, the lute chord accompanying the lowered fourth (a C♮, Figure 13, m. 2) is not Morley's printed A Major but rather a minor. The brighter A Major sonority and its tonicization of the dominant suits the printed version's sprightly textual imagery of merry lads playing

---

[100] Act II, *Minutum*, Morley, AVCAU Liber 321, f. 112r; Act II, Sutton (ed.), "The Intermedium *Minutum* (1613)." Thanks again to the reader who edited this translation.

[101] "Notis supra positis aptans." There is one other stanza of text for May written into the margin, "Silete, adeste caprigeni," which might have been added and sung to a different melody.

[102] L. Pike, *Pills to Purge Melancholy: The Evolution of the English Ballett* (Aldershot: Ashgate, 2004), 45–58.

[103] B. Ravelhofer, *The Early Stuart Masque: Dance, Costume and Music* (Oxford: Oxford University Press, 2006), 199–204.

Figure 9 First verse of "Iam lenis spirat aura," *Minutum* Act II, Thomas Morley. AVCAU Liber 321, f. 112r. Image copyright © the Venerable English College, Rome: reproduced with permission

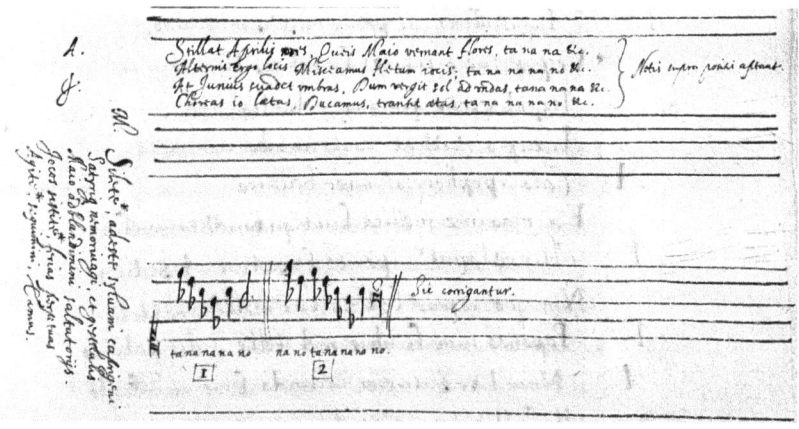

Figure 10 Other verses for and alterations to "Iam lenis spirat aura," f. 112r. Image copyright © the Venerable English College, Rome: reproduced with permission

(Figure 12, mm. 2–4). This British Library manuscript, however, remains more grounded in G, possibly to match the musical phrase's new text, "y^e wintrye stormes hath calmed." This could explain the same variant in the VEC

Figure 11 Transcription of "Iam lenis spirat aura," Verse 1, with scribe's original corrections (*) and author's proposed corrections (+)

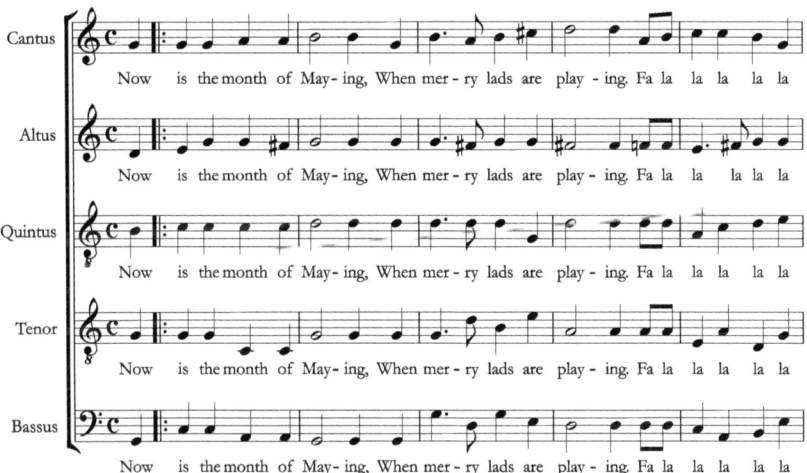

Figure 12 Transcription of Morley, "Now is the Month of Maying," Verse 1, *The First Booke of Balletts to Five Voyces*. London: Thomas Este, 1595

manuscript, as the analogous phrase in Liber 321 describes not energetic games but rather Flora's embrace of May as a gentle wind blows. When the VEC version later states, "us playful children of springtime," the C is then sharped and the fifth tonicized (Figure 11, m. 9). Similarly, in Add. MS 15117, the raised fourth is later introduced in the phrase, "To grace the lyvelye springe."[104]

Overall, the VEC version of Morley's melody is considerably more ornamented with Italianate divisions than its printed version (e.g. Figure 11, mm. 6,

---
[104] Add. MS. 15117, f. 10r, Gb-Lbl.

Figure 12 Cont.

7, and 15), and it also contains a handful of transcription mistakes. Both cadences are rewritten at the bottom of the page (Figure 10) next to the words "Thus these should be corrected."[105] These appear to be suggested ornaments, but there are in fact two rhythmic errors in the manuscript: The second syllable of "veris" is set on an eighth rather than a quarter note (Figures 9 and 11, m. 10),

---

[105] "Sic corrigantur." Act II, *Minutum*, Morley, AVCAU Liber 321, f. 112r; Act II, Sutton (ed.), "The Intermedium *Minutum* (1613)."

Figure 12 Cont

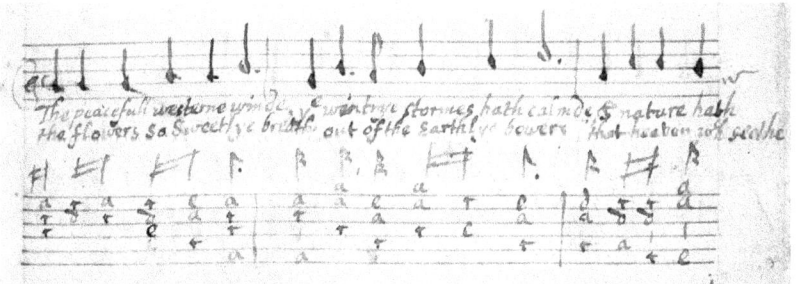

Figure 13 Excerpt of Morley, "The Peacefull Westerne Winde," Additional Manuscript 15117, f. 10r. British Library, London. British Library Board 2/1/2025.

and the melody over the final cadence seems rhythmically unviable in both its original and altered manuscript forms (Figures 9 and 11, mm. 14–15). As might have been the case with Wilbye's madrigal collections, Morley's book of balletts could have been held in the college library, or perhaps someone in the VEC community possessed a manuscript copy of the piece. It must not be discounted, however, that VEC scholars could have been working from memory without access to any notated music, which would perhaps explain the rhythmic errors in "Iam lenis spirat aura." This version also lacks Morley's printed repeats, only sounding each phrase once, which might have seemed more suitable for storytelling in a soloistic dramatic context.

These pieces, evidently performed by a group of solo singers, could have been accompanied by a lute, a viol consort, or any number of continuo instruments from the theorbo to the harpsichord. It is known that a violinist was paid to play in *S. Thomas Cantuariensis* and a harpsichordist was paid for *Zeno* when the *intermedio* was performed at the VEC again in 1634. Three different harpsichords were used for *Zeno*, one from the college music room and two rented from the Roman churches of Saint Cecilia in Trastevere and Sant'Isidoro a Capo le Case.[106] With their more homophonic texture, vertical harmonic structure, and greater emphasis on melody, English and Italian *balletti* alike were excellent candidates for performance as solo continuo songs. The tune for the less declamatory "Nuntie," however, with its several long pauses and sustained notes, perhaps indicates a more polyphonic relationship between singer and instrumental accompaniment.

Morley's writings on music draw clear distinctions between the Italianate madrigal and its lighter cousins, the canzonet and the ballett, while also acknowledging significant stylistic overlap between them. Unlike the madrigal, Morley specified, the strophic ballett was punctuated by "fa la" refrains and "devised to be daunced." In present-day music scholarship, the ballett is typically subsumed under the wider secular genre designation of "madrigal."[107] The college's players might have been aware of the ballett's indebtedness to Italian secular music, namely Morley's remodeling of Vecchi's *balletto* into "Now is the Month of Maying." Morley's ballett loosely follows the melodic contour of Vecchi's piece, shares its general phrase structure, and likewise includes a "fa la" refrain. The two pieces do sound markedly different, however. Most noticeably, Morley's piece is set in a major rather than minor mode, its text deals with a different topic, and it avoids Vecchi's half cadences to more frequently confirm the tonic. Vecchi's piece also starts off by repeating its initial phrase, "So ben mi c'ha bon tempo," both textually and musically, while Morley introduced a full couplet over two distinct musical phrases, "Now is the month of maying, when merry lads are playing." (Figure 12, mm. 1–4).[108]

The version of the ballet in VEC Liber 321 follows Morley's example more directly than that of Vecchi, for instance by beginning with the Latin couplet, "Iam lenis spirat aura, et Maium cingit Flora" over two separate musical phrases (Figure 11, mm. 1–4). However, more like Vecchi's piece, this manuscript version of the ballett melody, with its initial lowered fourth, does not drift into

---

[106] Gossett, "Drama in the English College, Rome, 1591–1660," 76–80.

[107] T. Murray, *Thomas Morley: Elizabethan Music Publisher* (Woodbridge: Boydell Press, 2014). 128–34.

[108] For this piece and its Italian model, see M. K. Long, "Characteristic Tonality in the *Balletti* of Gastoldi, Morley, and Hassler," *Journal of Music Theory* 59, no. 2 (2015): 235–71, and *Hearing Homophony: Tonal Expectation at the Turn of the Seventeenth Century* (Oxford: Oxford University Press, 2020); and Pike, *Pills to Purge Melancholy*, 39–58.

any other proto-tonal area in the first part of the piece. In this way, the English College version more closely aligns with Morley's Italian model. If the VEC version was indeed performed as a continuo song, its refrains would have likely lacked the elaborate polyphonic *stretto* imitation that differentiates Morley's printed ballett from Vecchi's more consistently homophonic piece (Figure 12, mm. 4–8 and 13–17). In the course of the ballett's "Latinization" for the VEC stage, both Vecchi's and Morley's original Italianate "fa la la" refrains were converted into "ta na no." *Minutum* presents both sets of nonsense syllables as musicalized birdsong. "Ta na no" is found more rarely in repertoires of the period, although it does appear in Wilbye's *Second Set of Madrigales*.[109]

Minutum's informal song contest indubitably carried many dimensions of meaning for the college's audiences. Songbirds such as cuckoos and nightingales make appearances in other Jesuit dramas of the time. *Dialogus Musicae* dramatized an inter-species birdsong competition as a symbolic commentary on Counter-Reformation debates about the merits of chant versus polyphony.[110] *Minutum* seems to have staged an analogous competition between polyphony ("Nuntie") and monody ("Iam lenis"). Early modern thinkers were intrigued by the relationship between birdsong and human music making, particularly by the possibility that the latter had evolved from the former. Some writers theorized that birdsong was an unadulterated form of sacred musical devotion and that animals shared a special rapport with the divine and the harmony of the spheres. In art, literature, and music, warbling songbirds came to symbolize extreme human suffering of a Christological nature.[111] In concordance with these themes, May sings of "god-greeting herons," whimpering blackbirds, and "sweet-complaining songbirds." Echo effects were also commonly heard in musical theatre on both sides of the Channel. Echoes had many dramatic functions; in Italian *intermedi*, echo effects were often deployed to evoke the harmony of the spheres and arouse a sense of wonder and bewilderment in spectator-auditors.[112] On the Roman Jesuit stage, however, echoes could also carry

---

[109] Thanks are due to one my two readers for pointing this out.
[110] Körndle, "Between Stage and Divine Service," 486–9.
[111] See L. P. Austern, "Nature, Culture, Myth, and the Musician in Early Modern England," *Journal of the American Musicological Society* 51, no. 1 (1998): 1–47; M. Lazarus, "Birdsongs and Sonnets: Acoustic Imitation in Renaissance Lyric," *Huntington Library Quarterly* 84, no. 4 (2021): 681–715; and C. Mahaffy, "'Melodious Madrigals': A Study of Animal Musicians in Early Modern England," *The Ben Jonson Journal* 27, no. 1 (2020): 126–43.
[112] For echo effects and *meraviglia* in Italian *intermedi*, see Treadwell, *Music and Wonder at the Medici Court* and "Music of the Gods." For echo effects in early modern English drama, see S. L. Anderson, *Echo and Meaning on Early Modern English Stages* (Cham: Palgrave Macmillan, 2018).

sinister connotations, representing a dark supernatural force or a character's own egoistic proclivity for sin.[113]

Minutum's echoes are not the path to success. June calls upon the natural world to send his voice back to him, but May knows better. May reverses the roles of imitator and imitated, instead altering his own voice to match the trilling of their avian companions. More than that, "Iam lenis" is proffered as a more successful piece of solo vocal music that distinguishes May's voice from other parts that June's voice merely "accompanies." May's singing pleases the "feathered choir," and soon, the birds, April, and June are all warbling May's ditty as well. In Italian musical theatre, bird-like nonsense syllables and other vocalized sounds were customarily deployed as markers of ethnic, racial, and religious difference. The birdsong topos more generally, with its proliferation of jargon, became a playful space in both English and mainland European secular music for sonic experimentation with acoustic imitation and translingualism.[114] Contrasted with June's more self-referential but less tuneful and declamatory vocal line, May's mimetic response to birdsong more closely approaches the Italian *stile moderno*. May pleases the birds not only by imitating their twittering but also by singing a more soloistic Italianate ballett emphasizing vertical sonorities.

This performance of a Latin-language, Italianate piece in an English *intermedio* remarking upon Becket's martyrdom insinuates a linkage between English adoption of Italian musical styles and an age-old English Catholicism stretching back to the medieval history of the Church. It has been proposed that Morley might have had Catholic sympathies, though this has never been confirmed.[115] "Nuntie" and "Iam lenis" could have shined a spotlight on the VEC as a distinctive local institution, as this repertoire was probably unknown to spectator-auditors. Stylistically, however, the "Latinized" ballett has much in common with Italian models; the VEC's foreign audiences might have heard an unrecognizable *balletto*, but it was a *balletto* all the same. More practically, the Latin contrafactum of "Iam lenis" undoubtedly helped to convey the *intermedio*'s plot to the college's foreign audiences.

In the context of both plays that the *intermedio* filled, *Minutum*'s birdsong and discourse about St. Thomas contrasted with the much less agreeable

---

[113] Lyon, "Magis corde quam organo," 169–70.
[114] See Lazarus, "Birdsongs and Sonnets"; G. Salvatore, "Parodie realistiche: Africanismi, fraternità e sentimenti identitari nelle canzoni moresche del Cinquecento," *Kronos* 14 (2012): 97–130; K. van Orden. "Music as a Sonic Record," *Huntington Library Quarterly* 82, no. 1 (2019): 17–42; and E. Wilbourne, "*Lo Schiavetto* (1612): Travestied Sound, Ethnic Performance, and the Eloquence of the Body," *Journal of the American Musicological Society* 63, no. 1 (2010): 1–44, *Seventeenth-Century Opera and the Sound of the Commedia dell'Arte*, and *Voice, Slavery, and Race in Seventeenth-Century Florence*.
[115] Murray, *Thomas Morley*, 14–19, 31–6.

fictional music making of the dramas' antagonists. Act II of *S. Thomas Cantuariensis* starts off with a dialogue about a martial ballet danced at the court of King Henry II (1133–89), described as a festive dance of Mars, the Greco-Roman god of war. The presiding King Henry, whose own courtiers will eventually assassinate Becket, is compared to a lion menacingly outstretched in the shade, keeping an eye on his court of beasts.[116] As explicated below, the bloodthirsty emperor in *Zeno* also engages in militaristic, decadent, and infernal musicking – nothing ever even close to the pleasant warbling of songbirds.

Minutum's audiences included the Cardinals Odoardo Farnese (1573–1626) in 1613 and Francesco Barberini (1597–1679) in 1634. Each was, in those respective years, designated as Cardinal Protector of the English College – or, in Carleton's sour words, "of the English fugitives." Aside from the pope, the college's cardinal protector was the institution's most significant patron, serving as the seminary's point of access into the papal court and wider Roman political networks. Any VEC play or sermon given before a college cardinal protector was a self-promotional opportunity to procure powerful support for the English mission.[117] Francesco Barberini was also the nephew of Pope Urban VIII, Maffeo Barberini. Farnese and Francesco Barberini were both important patrons of music in Rome who sponsored the staging of lavish musical dramas and the composition and performance of madrigals. Francesco Barberini was a viol enthusiast too. He maintained his own resident student viol consort for the playing of Italian madrigals under Mazzocchi's direction.[118]

Connecting with distinguished cardinals, Catholic ambassadors, and other foreign spectator-auditors was certainly an objective of these VEC productions, but the repeated singing and playing of English music also would have helped the college's priests-in-training to remain conversant with English musical repertoires in preparation for their return journeys across the Channel. English priests deployed contrafacta in Catholic evangelism by setting Latin religious texts to well-known English ballad and other profane tunes for covert spiritual instruction. Murphy has suggested that for recusant Catholics in England, subsequently hearing such popular melodies in public, even with secular vernacular texts, would have reinforced that earlier devotional messaging through

---

[116] Act II, Scenes 1–2, *S. Thomas Cantuariensis*, Sutton (ed.), "The Anonymous Tragedy *Thomas Cantuariensis* (1613)," *The Philological Museum* (updated October 12, 2004), https://philological.cal.bham.ac.uk/thomcant/.

[117] For cardinal protectors and VEC interactions with cardinals, see Underwood, "Representing England in Rome."

[118] Hammond, *Music & Spectacle in Baroque Rome*; M. Murata, "Barberini," in *Grove Music Online, Oxford Music Online* (2001), https://doi.org/10.1093/gmo/9781561592630.article.01998; F. Piperno, "Cardinals, Music, and Theatre," in M. Hollingsworth, M. Pattenden, and A. Witte (eds.), *A Companion to the Early Modern Cardinal* (Leiden: Brill, 2020), 600–15.

recalled association with the music's secret pedagogical use.[119] This twittering "Latinized" birdsong was a preparatory exercise for the English mission.

5 *Captiva Religio*, 1614

Captiva Religio, preserved in only two VEC manuscripts, draws on many different forms and styles of music to strike a contrast between the musicking of sacrilegious oppressors and of Catholic martyrs.[120] Unlike in other surviving college plays, however, the music of "heretics" in *Captiva* is not as frivolous as it first appears, and one specific musical instrument comes to represent the plight of English Catholic recusancy. This is the viol, an instrument that by 1614 was already loaded with symbolic meaning, especially in Britain. In *Captiva*, music made by the play's stereotypically wicked anti-Catholic characters reinforces a typecasting of heretical musicking as superficial and silly, while simultaneously foreshadowing the secret premeditated insurgence of these duplicitous buffoons against the ruling government. Once these clownish characters cast off their guises as symbolically Protestant antagonists and their true plans are revealed, their singing ceases and English Catholic martyrdom is "voiced" by the sound of a lamenting offstage viol.

Captiva's plotline centers the allegorical character of Religion, who has traveled to Protestant England to save its wayward people from the Reformation. Her mission is thwarted, however, when she is captured and tortured by the evil tyrant Archophylax, who orders her execution. Archophylax was a thinly veiled analogue of James I.[121] Just two years after *Captiva*'s revival in 1629, the character of Religion also appeared in the Roman martyr opera *Il Sant'Alessio*, by Stefano Landi, on the Barberini stage.[122] Religion's suffering lies at the heart of *Captiva*'s story, but never once does she speak or appear. Carleton vividly set the scene in his report to James I: *Captiva*'s story took place in London, with an edifice resembling the Tower "and other prisons filled wth priests and Jesuits, and in the middest the title of the play written in great gold Letters upon a Sanguin ground Captiva."[123] A Vatican Library fragment of one *argomento*, or program, for the 1629 revival

---

[119] Murphy, "Music and Catholic Culture in Post-Reformation Lancashire," 522–4.
[120] These manuscripts are AVCAU Liber 321 and Scrittura 33/3. Wiggins and Richardson, "1741. *Captiva* [The Female Captive]."
[121] Wiggins and Richardson, "1741. *Captiva* [The Female Captive]." See also Shell, *Catholicism, Controversy and the English Literary Imagination, 1558–1660*, 188–90, and D. Sutton (ed.), "The Anonymous Tragicomedy *Captiva Religio* (1614)," *The Philological Museum* (updated August 12, 2006), https://philological.cal.bham.ac.uk/capt/.
[122] M. Murata, "Allegorical Figures and Music' in Seventeenth-Century Spanish and Italian Scripts," in F. Antonucci and A. Tedesco (eds.), *La Comedia nueva e le scene italiane nel Seicento: Trame, drammaturgie, contesti a confronto*, (Florence: Leo S. Olschki, 2016), 179.
[123] Carleton to James I, February 11, 1614, State Papers 99/15, f. 83r, TNA.

relates that the action was first "stirred up by a Carnival Musician with a Clown, who then summon Comedy and Tragedy, and these ones conduct the Prologue."[124]

With Religion behind bars, Archophylax and his own clownish subjects celebrate their prisoner's death sentence with frenetic piping, fiddling, singing, dancing, and satyr ballets. In English and Italian theatre alike, satyr and other Bacchanal dances were emblematic of alcohol abuse, devilish incivility, and sexual predation.[125] The script mentions other conventionally pastoral, Bacchanalian instruments as well, namely the flute and lyre.[126] College accounts show that for the 1629 revival, a violinist and lutenist were paid and a tin whistle was purchased.[127] Federico Gotardi remarked that the entire 1614 production was "filled with ridiculous and clownish scenes."[128] In the *commedia dell'arte*, these shallow comic servant characters would have been classified as *zanni*.[129] Buffoonish *commedia*-inspired diversions were typical of Roman Jesuit school theatre, which vacillated between high and low forms of entertainment.[130] This production also featured an extraordinarily nimble cast member known for his acrobatic leaping, who had performed for James I as well.[131] In the Italian comic theatre, such acrobatics were commonly seen during *canario* and *sfessania* dances.[132]

All was not how it seemed, however, even in song. In Act I, Scene 3, the court jester Joculus sings what masquerades as a lighthearted tune about the Greco-Roman myth of Argus and Mercury, but little do the others realize that Joculus is, in fact, a crypto-Catholic whose real name is Ergastes. Religion will ultimately be released from imprisonment with his guileful assistance, just as the trickster Mercury successfully frees one of Jove's mortal love interests (disguised as a heifer) from captivity under the many-eyed giant Argus.[133] Italian

---

[124] "Excitatur á Musico Carnavale cum Macarone, que deinde Comaediam et Tragoediam evocant, illae Prologum agunt." MS Vaticani Latini 8263, Vol. 2, ff. 399r–v and 414v, Biblioteca Apostolica Vaticana, Vatican City. See Gossett, "Drama in the English College, Rome, 1591–1660"; Jakovac, "Performance Culture at the English College in Rome, *c.* 1579–1660"; and Wiggins and Richardson, "1741. Captiva [The Female Captive]."

[125] E. Nicholson, "Crossing Borders with Satyrs, the Irrepressible Genre-Benders of Pastoral Tragicomedy," *The Italianist* 40, no. 3 (2020): 342–61.

[126] Act I, Scenes 3 and 5, Act II, Scenes 2 and 4, Act III, Scenes 3 and 6, and Act IV, Scene 3, Sutton (ed.), "The Anonymous Tragicomedy *Captiva Religio* (1614)."

[127] Gossett, "Drama in the English College, Rome, 1591–1660," 69, 78.

[128] "... ripieni di scéne ridicule et buffonsche ..." Gotardi to Boncasio, February 15, 1614, State Papers 85/4, f. 101r–v, TNA.

[129] Wilbourne, *Seventeenth-Century Opera and the Sound of the Commedia dell'Arte*, 32–3.

[130] See Murata, "*Dal ridicolo al diletto signorile.*"

[131] Wiggins and Richardson, "1741. Captiva [The Female Captive]."

[132] Wilbourne, *Seventeenth-Century Opera and the Sound of the Commedia dell'Arte*, 43.

[133] Joculus (Ergastes), Act I, Scene 3, Sutton (ed.), "The Anonymous Tragicomedy *Captiva Religio* (1614)."

Figure 14 "Argus centoculatus," *Captiva Religio* (1614) Act I, Scene 3. AVCAU Liber 321, f. 129r. Image copyright © the Venerable English College, Rome: reproduced with permission

audiences probably clocked Joculus as falling into another specific *commedia dell'arte* category: that of the *primo zanni*, or the clever mastermind of the *zanni*, often an incognito protagonist pursuing his own secret plot. Disguise was a common denominator in most *commedia zanni* storylines.[134]

The melody given for Joculus's piece (Figures 14 and 15) is a well-traveled French tune of the era, "Une jeune pucelle." By 1614 the song was known throughout Italy and England, and in the 1640s a French Jesuit missionary and martyr in North America, Jean de Brébeuf, also set the tune to the Wendat language in the famed Huron Carol, "Jesous Ahatonnia."[135] In *commedia* theatre, popular song repertoires with contrafacta were usually the domain of *zanni*. The VEC's audiences might have recognized the melody and understood its applicability to Joculus's character type. Ecclesiastical spectator-auditors might have heard it as a sly nod to Jesuit practices of devising religious Latin contrafacta for secular songs. The piece's "fa la" refrain was also an appropriate marker of the jester's social station, as lower-class *commedia* characters tended to sing nonsense syllables.[136]

---

[134] Wilbourne, *Seventeenth-Century Opera and the Sound of the Commedia dell'Arte*, 32–3.

[135] Many thanks to expert tune detective Ross Duffin for identifying this piece. K. Stilwell, "Adopting Rituals: The Jesuits and the Huron Noël, 'Jesous Ahatonnia'," in A. H. Celenza and A. R. DelDonna (eds.), *Music as Cultural Mission: Explorations of Jesuit Practices in Italy and North America* (Philadelphia: Saint Joseph's University Press, 2014), 143–61; J. Wendland, "'Madre non mi far Monaca': The Biography of a Renaissance Folksong," *Acta Musicologica* 48, no. 2 (1976): 185–204.

[136] Wilbourne, *Seventeenth-Century Opera and the Sound of the Commedia dell'Arte*, 42–4.

Figure 15 Transcription of "Argus centoculatus," Verse 1

Argus centoculatus,	*Hundred-eyed Argus,*
Fa la la &c.	*Fa la la &c.*
Iuvencae custos datus,	*Was made to guard a heifer,*
Fa la la &c.	*Fa la la &c.*
Mercurius dolosus,	*Sneaky Mercury,*
Custodem est perosus,	*Hated this guard,*
Fit Argus somniculosus	*And Argus grew sleepy,*
Fa la la &c.	*Fa la la &c.*[137]

The play's more superficial musicking is eventually turned on its head to help liberate Religion. In Act IV another crypto-Catholic, Philaretus, and his servant Eutrapelus together attempt to persuade three different local magistrates to stay away from Religion's execution. The final magistrate they visit is the Protestant parson Prurio, who throughout the drama had enthusiastically played the "screeching" fiddle and participated in satyr dances. Philaretus and Eutrapelus accuse the cleric of impiety in his music making, trying to convince him that he will be forced into public penance if he attends the execution:

EUTRAPELUS: Oh you false-speaking, foolish-speaking, silly-speaking man! You who sowed these crimes will reap them presently. For ... did you play that screeching fiddle of yours while the chaplains, luxuriating in their wanton carriage, aped satyrs with their dancing?

PRURIO: I'm not ashamed of the deed.

EUTRAPELUS: But you ought to be ashamed. This arouses everybody's bile, for you to celebrate other people's misfortunes with games, and for you, who serve as a model, to set yourself up to be imitated in disgraceful things.[138]

---

[137] Many thanks again to one of my reviewers for editing this translation. Joculus, Act I, Scene 3, *Captiva Religio*, AVCAU Liber 321, f. 129r; Sutton (ed.), "The Anonymous Tragicomedy *Captiva Religio* (1614)."

[138] Act IV, Scene 4, Sutton (ed.), "The Anonymous Tragicomedy *Captiva Religio* (1614)."

In the final act of *Captiva*, just before Religion is unexpectedly spared from death, Ergastes delivers a sorrowful monologue mourning the sad fate of both Religion and England. His words are interrupted when he hears the sound of a "throbbing viol" coming from Religion's prison cell. The instrument might have been played by one of the interned English Catholic characters clustered together on-stage. Moved by this music, Ergastes declares that Religion is playing her own swan song, an Italian "song of Faith" (possibly a hymn) to the crucified Christ, and he compares the viol's timbre to the human voices of Catholics in Rome with whom he had formerly bewailed the Crucifixion. His language implies that these lamenting voices were a figurative viol played by God:

> (*Falling to his knees.*) Farewell, Captive, farewell Religion. Prison and sweet chains which bind the Captive, Farewell. And you, you holy hinges and you scaffold, destined soon to bear Religion, farewell you all. (*Stands.*) And you, England, who will never cease your funereal groaning, farewell. Already torn away from all the world, now you will be sung of as having been torn away from the light of heaven. Then I, returned, (*A viol throbs within.*) What do I hear? Thus it is, a swan-song, the Captive is singing her own funeral dirges. Ah how often at Rome, with the very same sounds which he would summon forth with his viol, we humbly bewailed with our sad voices the sorrows of the Cross! (*On the throbbing viol is played within an Italian song of faith to the crucified Lord. When it is played, he goes to the gate.*) Captive, I cannot control myself lest my final grieving word issue forth. Captive Religion, this is Ergastes.[139]

This serious soliloquy is a departure from the jester's earlier comic register. Joculus sings; Ergastes does not. Ergastes instead speaks eloquently while Religion produces poignant sacred music in the background. Set against the tragicomedy's earlier throng of rustic instruments and secular sonic pleasures, this comparatively sober sacred musical offering on a more sophisticated instrument transforms Ergastes and his co-conspirators from godless rascals into saintly saviors of their nation. In this moment, both English Catholics and their "Captive Religion" are represented by an Italian dirge on the viol, an Italianate instrument that by 1614 had accrued numerous dimensions of cultural meaning throughout early modern Europe.

In Tudor England, the viol was initially characterized as an Italian import, but the instrument quickly transformed into a strong emblem of English cultural identity, both at home and abroad. A high number of virtuosic English violists traveling the Continent – many of them Catholic – received

---

[139] "Pulsatae int' fidei cantilenam + admodulatur verbis Italiacis de crucifixo Domino concinnatam." I have slightly amended Sutton's translation of the stage directions to provide a clearer translation of the viol's role in the scene. Joculus (Ergastes), Act V, Scene 1, *Captiva Religio*, AVCAU Liber 321, f. 167r–v; Sutton (ed.), "The Anonymous Tragicomedy *Captiva Religio* (1614)."

a great deal of attention and student consort performance was recognized as a distinctively English practice.[140] In England the instrument had been closely linked to education since the mid-sixteenth century, as it was common in choir schools for companies of young boys to play in viol consorts, often performing at important public events.[141] This pedagogical practice extended into English Jesuit educational networks. More generally, the viol had long been viewed in both Italy and England as a symbol of aristocratic refinement and erudition. Instruction on the viol was thought an ideal means of training the bodies and souls of young elites to participate in upper-class, cosmopolitan sociability.[142] The viol's timbre was famously likened to that of the human voice, but in Elizabethan England, associations between the viol and human body-soul were intensified as the instrument was feminized and eroticized in literary sources, compared directly to female characters or to the physical body of a player's sexual partner. The instrument could symbolize sexual promiscuity as much as a virginal purity aligned with the godly perfection of *musica mundana*.[143] The English viol and its consorts were also heavily associated with death, grief, and the physio-spiritual melancholic affliction, particularly after Protestant injunctions against rituals of mourning had restricted collective demonstrations of grief in Tudor England; playing melancholic music in consort was an outlet for shared expressions of sorrow. For English Catholics, viol repertoires also allowed for participation in suppressed devotional practices, for example through the playing of *In nomine* and *Miserere mihi* cantus firmus settings.[144]

The early modern viol was frequently subject to anthropomorphism, but the pulsating heart of *Captiva*'s tortured "viol" gestures specifically toward what Jonathan Gibson has termed "corporeal indexing," or an objectification of human body parts through their identification with various parts of an instrument. Such metaphorical constructions tended to privilege grotesque imagery of physical sickness, pain, and death. One seventeenth-century English ballad, for

---

[140] del Amo Iribarren, "Anthony Poole (c.1629–1692), the Viol and Exiled English Catholics."
[141] I. Woodfield, *The Early History of the Viol* (Cambridge: Cambridge University Press, 1984), 212–27.
[142] R. Ahrendt, "The Diplomatic Viol," in F. Ramel and C. Prévost-Thomas (eds.), *International Relations, Music and Diplomacy: Sounds and Voices on the International Stage* (Cham: Palgrave Macmillan, 2018), 93–114; C. Marsh, *Music and Society in Early Modern England* (Cambridge: Cambridge University Press, 2010), 173–224; A. Otterstedt, *The Viol: History of an Instrument* (Kassel: Bärenreiter, 2002); and Woodfield, *The Early History of the Viol*.
[143] L. Ludwig, "'Equal to All Alike': A Cultural History of the Viol Consort in England, c. 1550–1675," unpublished Ph.D. diss., University of Virginia (2011), 211–70; G. Ungerer, "The Viol da Gamba as a Sexual Metaphor in Elizabethan Music and Literature," *Renaissance and Reformation* 8, no. 2 (1984): 79–80; and C. R. Wilson, *Shakespeare's Musical Imagery* (London: Bloomsbury, 2015).
[144] Ludwig, "Equal to All Alike," 31–91, 135–210.

example, "The Miller and the King's Daughter," narrates a harrowing story in which a princess is murdered and an unscrupulous miller who finds her corpse fashions different parts of the cadaver into a viol: her breastbone becomes the main instrument, her fingers become its pegs, her nose its bridge, and her veins its strings. When the miller plays this viol, the woman's dismembered body is gruesomely reanimated. Her shins dance, evoking the *danse macabre*, and the instrument "sings" to reveal that the princess's murderer was none other than her elder sister. Gibson has analyzed further, more Christological instances of viol anthropomorphism and corporeal indexing in J.S. Bach's *St. Matthew Passion*, in which the instrument is sounded during passages of text referring to the cross and agonized body of Christ.[145]

In *Captiva*, Ergastes transmutes these diverse cultural associations with the viol into a brief ponderance on the Holy Trinity and the crucified body of Christ as they are incarnated within the nobly suffering, music-making body of the English Catholic martyr, or the beating heart of God himself. *Captiva's* throbbing viol, anthropomorphized as the imprisoned Catholic Religion, endures Christological anguish at the hands of the English government. And, like the king's daughter in "The Miller," Religion's own voice is heard only once she is metamorphosed into a musical instrument. The martyrs that she represents may not be able to express their own grief through music, but the feminized Religion ventriloquizes their lamentations by "singing" an Italian sacred song of mourning for the fate of her nation on the plaintive viol, an Italianate but also, paradoxically, markedly English instrument.

It is no wonder that the staunchly Protestant ambassador Dudley Carleton was not thrilled with this play.[146] He accused the college's students of "diffaming their Countrey and nation wth representations of fained persecutions w[ch] they would make the Romans beleave they suffer in England." The disgraceful tragicomedy had concluded, Carleton informed the king, "wth a daunce or a jigg."[147] About one month later, the archbishop Abbot responded to Carleton's report with a threatening message:

> I do not marvell, that our Jesuites at Rome do sett out such foolish playes, for Owen their Rectour is but a blockhead, and commonly as the forehorse leadeth, so the rest will follow. I never tooke delight in spilling of bloud,

---

[145] J. Gibson, "Hearing the Viola da Gamba in 'Komm, süsses Kreuz'," in C. Fontijn and S. Parisi (eds.), *Fiori musicali: Liber amicorum Alexander Silbiger* (Sterling Heights: Harmonie Park Press, 2010), 419–50. I presented a still-unpublished paper on the "Miller" ballad at the 2015 McGill University Schulich School of Music Graduate Symposium: "'Music is my Mistress': The Undead Viol as a Source of Ghoulish Humor in *The Miller and the King's Daughter*."

[146] For Carleton's views on Catholic music, see my "Singing Nuns and Soft Power: British Diplomats as Music Tourists in Seicento Venice," *Religions* 13, no. 4 (2022): 330–44.

[147] Carleton to James I, February 11, 1614, State Papers 99/15, f. 83r–v, TNA.

but the insolencies of such persons at home and abrode, doth deserve some deeper castigation, then heere is layd upon them. [148]

6 *Roffensis*, 1615

No music survives for the Latin tragedy *Roffensis*, again about the Henrician Reformation and performed at the college six times in 1615, but the play's script does represent an obvious rift between Catholic and heretical music making. The drama's author is unknown, and its text survives only in Liber 321. Its connected *intermedio*, *Sensus, Fronto, Somnium*, includes musical staves for a sinfonia, but that music is now lost. The drama's unsinging protagonist is John Fisher (1469–1535), the English cardinal and Bishop of Rochester who was executed by the Tudor government.[149] *Roffensis* begins with jovial preparations for the marriage of Henry VIII to Anne Boleyn, during which a courtier named Bryan remarks in Act I, Scene 2,

> Now Catherine [of Aragon] is succumbing to old age, while Anne is in her green years. And Anne strums her sonorous lute, dances to music, enters easily into joking, and gently governs her serene face, adroit at producing laughter and well-chosen tears. Whereas Catherine bathes her cheeks with genuine downpours, she drags out deep sighs, she implores, she groans, so that with her prayers she might placate a hostile God.[150]

In Bryan's view, Catherine of Aragon's heartfelt sighs, groans, and prayers to God are no match for the younger Boleyn's calculated, musically inflected social graces. Bryan's words ascribe a charming superficiality to Boleyn's dancing and lute playing. Her music is sonorous, but it is principally a tool for seduction that has ensnared the king in a destructive haze of erotomania.[151] These two feminine musical stereotypes were ingrained within *commedia dell'arte* and English dramatic traditions. Catherine falls into the abandoned and lamenting *prima donna innamorata* character type, while Boleyn is the more ardent, courtesan-like *seconda donna innamorata*.[152] On the English

---

[148] Abbot to Carleton, March 16, 1614, State Papers 14/76, f. 98r, TNA.
[149] AVCAU Liber 321, *Roffensis*, f. 225r. See Jakovac, "Performance Culture at the English College in Rome, *c.* 1579–1660"; D. Sutton (ed.), "The Anonymous Tragedy *Roffensis*," *The Philological Museum* (updated February 27, 2013), https://philological.cal.bham.ac.uk/roff/; and Wiggins and Richardson, "1863. *Roffensis* [Rochester]" and "1864. *Sensus, Fronto, Somnoum* [Sense, Blow, Dream]," in *British Drama 1533-1642*, Vol. 7 (2016).
[150] Bryan, Act I, Scene 2, Sutton (ed.), "The Anonymous Tragedy *Roffensis*."
[151] This became a wider trope about Anne Boleyn's musicking. See L.P. Austern, "Anne Boleyn, Musician: A Romance Across Centuries and Media" in J. Fitzmaurice, N. J. Miller, and S. Steen (eds.), *Authorizing Early Modern European Women from Biography to Biofiction* (Amsterdam: Amsterdam University Press, 2022), 141–56.
[152] See Wilbourne, *Seventeenth-Century Opera and the Sound of the Commedia dell'Arte*.

stage, the two equivalent archetypes would have been the plaintive fallen wife and the capricious courtesan whose beguiling musical talents served an ulterior motive.[153] Catherine, like the English martyr, does not sing.

Bryan's comparison of the two women is followed, unsurprisingly, by the presentation of an armed ensemble dance to entertain the wedding party, attended also by the allegorical character of Madness. The king's arrival is heralded by a trumpet.[154] By the second act of *Roffensis*, however, music making no longer belongs solely to the reigning government, shifting instead into a nobler, more somber space of lamentation for the Catholic martyr. A sorrowful chorus of nations voices their support for Fisher, contrasting the king's musical glorification with the relative lack of praise that Fisher has received. Rome asks the bishop, " [W]ho will be your herald? What trumpet will celebrate you, Rochester, glory of your nation and excellent shepherd of your flock?" Germany declares Fisher's opposition to the king's second marriage a "deed worthy of a perpetual trumpet." England and Spain foretell that gods and bards will sing of Fisher's virtue in years to come.[155] In Act IV these same nations proclaim that their lands and people will mourn Fisher's martyrdom in song.[156] This allegorical choir of nations weaves the character of Catholic England into its musical texture, perhaps gesturing toward a pan-European religio-cultural front.

When Fisher's severed head is gruesomely displayed in the play's final scene, Henry VIII still has only warlike music on the mind, warning, "And let the North be the first to feel my threats ... if their public bugle sounds any opposition, and their sharp furor and impious hot-headedness makes a noise."[157] Madness (who identifies Henry VIII as his patron) responds to the king's aggression with a "song" reflecting on the sad state of England. Its text has all the hallmarks of stereotypical demonic noise making, associated directly with the heretical king:

> Throw open the recesses of Hell's heaven, you bevy of three Sister [sic], let victorious Orcus roar with happy bellows ... With piety put to rout, I sing of my patron and of the conquered faith, and of a fraternal army consumed by civil strife ..., of the government of Avernus extended, of England submitting to the laws of great Dis, and of their tyrant being placed under the Furies' bridle.[158]

---

[153] See K. K. Wong, *Music and Gender in English Renaissance Drama* (London: Routledge, 2013), 23–46.
[154] Act I, Scene 3, Sutton (ed.), "The Anonymous Tragedy *Roffensis*."
[155] Second Chorus, Act II, Sutton (ed.), "The Anonymous Tragedy *Roffensis*."
[156] Fourth Chorus, Act IV, Sutton (ed.), "The Anonymous Tragedy *Roffensis*."
[157] King Henry VIII, Act V, Scene 4, Sutton (ed.), "The Anonymous Tragedy *Roffensis*."
[158] Madness, Act V, Scene 4, Sutton (ed.), "The Anonymous Tragedy *Roffensis*."

7 English-Language Plays, 1633–1635

Two English-language plays performed at the VEC in the 1630s, *The New Moon* and *Comedy of Geometry*, apparently featured a great variety of music. The former (author unknown) only appears in one VEC manuscript source, Scrittura 35/2, and was staged at the college in 1633. It stands out from most other known English College plays in that it defies a number of Jesuit conventions: It is a secular pastoral comedy, is written in English, and stars a female character. Its plot follows a conflict between Cynthia, a mythological personification of the moon, and her brother Phoebus, the sun. Phoebus deliberates whether to withhold his usual monthly supply of light to Cynthia, who has been accused of many misdoings. He convenes a senate of gods to help him decide his sister's fate. The character of Cynthia would have been played by a male actor, a dramatic practice that persisted within the society despite attempts by Jesuit generals to forbid it.[159] Gossett has proposed that *The New Moon* might have been reserved for an English-speaking audience.

In Act I, Scene 2 of *The New Moon*, the Greco-Roman god Vulcan and two of his cyclops apprentices sing a tune for the god Mercury, "Amongst the Gods Great Vulcan Swayeth." Marginalia for the song text specify that the piece was sung to an air by Morley, though the script includes no musical notation. Judging from its "fa la" refrain, this text was probably set to another of Morley's ballett melodies. This production could have featured any of the instrumental configurations proposed for *Thomas Morus* and *Minutum*, but college accounts do specify that VEC expenses for *The New Moon* went toward a small harp and the refurbishment, stringing, and tuning of a harpsichord. The script also indicates that the singers of this piece were accompanied by a lute or cittern and the percussive sound of beating hammers. This scene might have derived from an earlier English court masque, Ben Jonson's 1608 *The Fugitive Cupid* (a.k.a. the *Haddington Masque*), in which Vulcan's cyclopes beat time with their hammers to dance music composed by Alfonso Ferrabosco II.[160] Such scenes were also

---

[159] *The New Moon*, AVCAU Scrittura 35/2. See Gossett, "Drama in the English College, Rome, 1591–1660," 60–2, 71–4; M. Saulini, "Twenty-Five Years of Research on Jesuit Drama: An Italian Contribution to the History of Theatre" in A. Farkas and G. Körömi (eds.), *Új eredmények a színház- és drámatörténeti kutatásban (17–19. század): Tanulmányok a dráma- és színháztörténet köréből* (Eger: Eszterházy Károly Katolikus Egyetem Líceum Kiadó, 2022), 148–9; and Wiggins and Richardson, "2397. The New Moon," in *British Drama 1533–1642*, Vol. 9 (2018).

[160] Gossett, "Drama in the English College, Rome, 1591–1660," 76–80; Wiggins and Richardson, "1584. Court Wedding Masque: The Fugitive Cupid," in *British Drama 1533–1642*, Vol. 5 (2015) and "2397. The New Moon."

typical of contemporary court entertainments in Savoy.[161] *The New Moon*'s text for the corresponding Morley piece is as follows:

> Amongst the Goddes great Vulcan swayeth,
> Whose awfull hammerres the world obayeth: fa la la.
>
> Earth, fyre, ayre, water, with forge he scareth,
> Lead, tynne, brasse, iron, with knockes he teareth. fa la la.
>
> Jove with his wanton Juno danceth.
> Phebus his coursers up and downe pranceth: fa. la. la.
>
> Old Saturne sleepeth, Mars blowes is dealinge,
> Cynthia weepeth, Mercurie is stealinge fa la la.
>
> Then live God Vulcan singe we ever,
> Till old blinde Chaos the heavenes dissever: fa la la.
>
> Whose brave Cyclopes, when they are weary,
> Quaffe boles of nectar, dance and are merry. fa la la,[162]

One musical setting does survive for *The New Moon*, "The Nightingale that Sits," sung in Act III, Scene 6 by Crepusculum, the servant of a choleric elderly man. This is the ballad melody "Rogero," which was known in England but seems to have originated on the Continent as a popular ground bass for the improvisation of Italian poetry. Its first documented appearance was in the second book of the Spanish composer and music theorist Diego Ortiz's *Trattado de glosas* (Rome: Valerio and Luigi Dorico, 1553).[163] Whether or not audiences for this piece were English, the Italianate tune probably would have sounded familiar. Crepusculum sings this strophic, syllabic song in an attempt to melt the hard heart of Phoebus in Cynthia's favor. It was duetted by a pipe.[164] It also seems that the final line of each sung stanza was followed by an extra spoken or sung phrase of text, maybe as an echo (Figures 16 and 17):

> The Nightingall that sittes
> With brest against a thorne,

---

[161] See C. Santarelli, *La gara degli elementi: Acqua, aria, terra, e fuoco nelle feste sabaude (1585–1699)* (Lucca: Libreria Musicale Italiana, 2010).

[162] Act I, Scene 2, *The New Moon*, AVCAU Scrittura 35/2, ff. 5v–6r.

[163] Thank you to Ross Duffin for also identifying this piece. For "Rogero" see R. W. Duffin, "Framing a Ditty for Elizabeth: Thoughts on Music for the 1602 Summer Progress," *Early Music History* 2020, no. 39 (2020): 115–48, and *Some Other Note: The Lost Songs of English Renaissance Comedy* (Oxford: Oxford University Press, 2018); and J. Ward, "Music for *A Handefull of Pleasant Delites*," *Journal of the American Musicological Society* 10, no. 3 (1957): 151–80.

[164] de Kisch, "Fêtes et representations au Collège Anglais de Rome 1612–1614," 532; Wiggins and Richardson, "2397. *The New Moon*."

English Madrigals on the Jesuit Stage

Figure 16 Melody for "The Nightingale that Sits," *The New Moon* (1633) Act III, Scene 6. AVCAU Scrittura 35/2, f. 46r. Image copyright © the Venerable English College, Rome: reproduced with permission

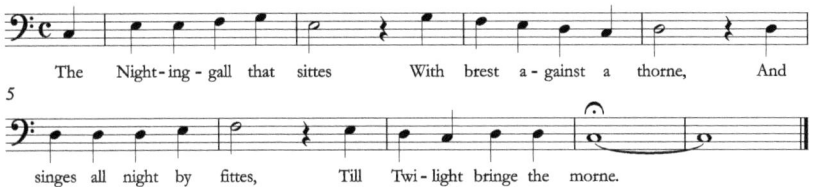

Figure 17 Transcription of "The Nightingale that Sits," Verse 1

And singes all night by fittes,
Till Twilight bringe the morne. (Twilight, that's I.)

When first she me espies,
Her note doth pierce myne eare,
And biddes me wipe myne eyes,
That have not shedd a teare. (Sorrow will out someway.)

Then if dame Cynthia appeeres,
Of nightly lampes the chiefe:
Her moonefull voyce she cleeres,
And danceth round for griefe. (O the strange effect of anguish.)

But now her light is dunne,
That we in darke must sleepe:
Which makes me curse hir Sunne,
And say the Goddes him keepe. (I am resolvd heereafter to be
  merry in the darke, and to sleepe soundly.)[165]

Throughout the play, Crepusculum and another servant, Pygmalion, attempt to placate the stubborn Phoebus by entertaining him with music, dancing, sports,

---

[165] Crepusculum, Act III, Scene 6, *The New Moon*, AVCAU Scrittura 35/2, f. 46r–v; Wiggins and Richardson, "2397. *The New Moon*."

and jokes. Pygmalion plays the pipe and Pan stages a satyr ballet. The still-judgmental Phoebus, however, remains unimpressed with these worldly delights, relenting only when moved to pity by both Cynthia's tears and Crepusculum's sweet song.[166] This heartrending music and the strong penitent response that it elicits from Phoebus evoke records of tearful audience responses to English martyr dramas and the typical denouements of those plays, especially in scripts in which the melodious chirruping of angelic "songbirds" is contrasted with the cacophony of heretics. In much early modern religious discourse, the nightingale symbolized the Virgin Mary and martyrological devotion.[167] These connotations are accentuated in the play by Crepusculum's narration of the bird warbling in grief with her breast against a thorn.

References to Cynthia and Phoebus appear in multiple VEC martyr plays as well. The siblings are usually portrayed as oppositional, representational forces. In Act II of *Thomas Morus*, for example, a chorus sings that "Cynthia, shining with her wandering and ever-changing face, indicates the king of England [Henry VIII] has a deceitful heart."[168] In *Mercia,* the VEC play that most literally praises a sweet songbird, the drama's wicked Pagan characters even worship Phoebus in song, scandalizing the play's Christian characters. In the first act, the Christian bishop Saint Chad warns, "Put no trust in Phoebus; he's a liar."[169] In Act IV a brigand on the run from the wrath of *Mercia*'s tyrannical, sun-worshipping Pagan king justifies his own marauding by proclaiming that "[t]he moon steals light from Phoebus," and "[t]he notorious thieving of kings escapes punishment; these great plunderers of possessions carry off spoils with impunity, while crosses await the thieving of the ordinary folk."[170]

Another English-language play entitled *Comedy of Geometry* (a.k.a. *Blame Not Our Author*), preserved only in VEC manuscript Scrittura 35/1, might have been staged for a small anglophone audience at the college or inserted as an *intermedio* within a longer play there, most likely in 1635. The plot winds its way through a series of amusing conflicts between different Plautine geometric shapes and tools, for example the characters Quadro, Compass, and Rectangulum.[171] In Act I, Scene 3, Quadro hears music and attempts to dance

---

[166] Wiggins and Richardson, "2397. *The New Moon.*"
[167] See Austern, "Nature, Culture, Myth, and the Musician in Early Modern England."
[168] Chorus, Act II, Scene 3, Sutton (ed.), "The Anonymous Tragedy *Thomas Morus* (1612)."
[169] Ceadda, Act I, Scene 3, *Mercia*, trans. R. F. Grady in L. J. Oldani and P.C. Fischer (eds.), *Jesuit Theatre Englished: Five Tragedies of Joseph Simons* (St. Louis: The Institute of Jesuit Sources, 1989), 86.
[170] Chorebus, Act IV, Scene 2, *Mercia*, trans. Grady in Oldani and Fischer (eds.), *Jesuit Theatre Englished*, 124–5.
[171] Thank you to Maurice Whitehead for providing further information to help with the approximate dating of the play. This dating is based on an opening inscription in the play's manuscript which names a "Thomas Turrettus," an alias for a student at the college named Thomas

but cannot do so, as Compass, his creator, has bound him in hoops to help him transform his shape into a circle. The tune played was "Sellinger's Round," a popular country dance melody in England at the time, thought to be of Irish origin. Several arrangements survive, including one by William Byrd.[172]

Compass refers to the instrument constraining Quadro as the "Squarenigher's daughter," an allusion to a real instrument of torture, the Scavenger's daughter, which had been used to compress the bodies of Catholic prisoners in Tudor England. *Comedy of Geometry* makes multiple references to physical violence perpetrated against Catholics. In following with the Catholic martyr archetype, the melancholic Quadro is righteous and self-disciplined, willing to endure the discomfort of contorting his own body in hopes of attaining the perfection of a circular form.[173] In Jesuit pedagogy, geometrical entrainment of the body through music and dance was encouraged as a moralizing exercise that disciplined students into achieving greater physical and spiritual alignment with the ideal mathematical proportions of the harmony of the spheres.[174] In English theatre, country dances such as "Sellinger's Round" were typically performed during antimasques featuring undignified, low-class characters.[175] By restraining himself from joining in on this dance number, Quadro chooses a nobler spiritual path than the other shapes have followed.

By contrast, Quadro's devious servant Rectangulum is more self-serving and dives into morally questionable schemes. He sings a long drinking song in Act II, Scene 6, "Bring the Juice of Hebe." No music survives. Drinking songs in Jesuit theatre were not performed without controversy. They were sometimes

---

Babthorpe. Babthorpe entered the college in October 1634 and in October 1635 left the VEC to enter the Roman Jesuit novitiate at the church of Sant'Andrea al Quirinale. Supposing that Babthorpe was involved in the play, the only possible window for his participation would have been between late 1634 and late 1635. The most likely possibility is that this play is the unnamed 1635 Shrovetide comedy listed in VEC archival records. See S. Gossett (ed.), "*Blame Not Our Author,* from the MS (Scrittura 35.1) at the Venerable English College, Rome," *Malone Society Collections* 2 (1983): 85–132; C. Mazzio, "The Three-Dimensional Self: Geometry, Melancholy, Drama," in D. Glimp and M. R. Warren (eds.), *Arts of Calculation: Quantifying Thought in Early Modern Europe* (New York: Palgrave Macmillan, 2004), 39–65; Y. Nasifoglu, "Embodied Geometry in Early Modern Theatre" in M. Pitici (ed.), *The Best Writing on Mathematics 2021* (Princeton: Princeton University Press, 2022), 77–81; D. Sutton (ed.), "The Jesuit Playlet *Blame Not Our Author,*" *The Philological Museum* (updated November 2, 2021), https://philological.cal.bham.ac.uk/blamenot/; B. Wardhaugh, *Encounters with Euclid: How an Ancient Greek Geometry Text Shaped the World* (Princeton: Princeton University Press, 2021), 145–50; and Wiggins and Richardson, "2467. *Comedy of Geometry*" in *British Drama 1533-1642*, Vol. 9.

[172] See "Sellinger's Round [1]," *Traditional Tune Archive* (updated August 7, 2020), https://tunearch.org/wiki/Annotation:Sellinger%27s_Round_(1).

[173] Nasifoglu, "Embodied Geometry in Early Modern Theatre," 79–81.

[174] van Orden, *Music, Discipline, and Arms in Early Modern France,* 37–80.

[175] Ravelhofer, *The Early Stuart Masque,* 43–4, 67–71.

prohibited by college leadership for their celebration of impropriety, even if the character singing them on-stage was a villain.[176]

> Bring the juice of Hebe,
> Chase away sadnesse dull.
> Pring [sic] the sweet Nepenthe,
> Fill the bowle up to be the full.
> Straw sweet flowers,
> Springle the ground
> With sweet bramble till we ramble
> And drinke in a round.
> Come come come bring forth the ale,
> Brown as berry. Let's bee merry
> Least our nose looks pale.
>
> *Downe downe downe* &c.
> Bacchus doth blow us a merry fresh gale.
> *Downe downe downe* &c.
> Leet us carowse the jolly bocale.
>
> Bring the rosy alligant,
> Choyse as that Vulcan drinks.
> Mauger hell and termagent
> Fill the cupp to the brincke.
> Come fayre nymphes, crowne of delight,
> Take your labor with your tabor
> To play Bacchus' right.
> Quaff and laff until our heeles
> Gin to stager and we swager
> Till our body reeles.
>
> *Downe downe downe* &c.
> Now do my nimble tongue caper on wheeles
> *Downe downe downe* &c.
> He that carouses no sorrowe hee feeles.
>
> Crowne our heads with nectar
> Till the moone call forth the night
> And the fayre Hyperion
> Shaded hath this clear light.
> Fairy gods come forth your hills,
> Trip with pleasure, daunce the measure that all sorrow kills.
> Bowze the can till wee goe round
> And Rectangle gins to wrangle and falls on the ground.
> Nere a good fellow but drinks till he's swound

---

[176] Körndle, "Between Stage and Divine Service," 481–2.

Downe downe downe &c.
Come bring the bugle to tipple profound.[177]

Even if *The New Moon* and *Comedy of Geometry* were performed for a polyglot audience, their insertion of additional English pieces beyond Italianate madrigals and balletts seems designed to appeal to English musical tastes. Even so, like Morley's balletts, "Rogero" was itself rooted in a Continental musical prototype. It is possible that VEC seminarians endeavored to secure support from visiting English patrons during this time and so tailored these performances to better reflect musico-dramatic practices in Britain. Morley's compositions, "Rogero," and "Sellinger's Round" were doubtless recognizable to many English ears by the 1630s, which could have brought delight to listeners desiring to feel at home in a foreign land. If performed for more international audiences, however, these productions could have introduced a variety of new English repertoires into the theatrical culture of Seicento Rome.

8 Tragedies by Joseph Simons, 1634–1648

College plays from the 1630s onward seem to have abandoned Reformation England as a standard dramatic setting, but many of the same sonic characterizations of Christian martyrs and their adversaries from earlier VEC dramas did continue to resonate in college productions from the Caroline and Civil War periods. This is certainly the case in a handful of Latin tragedies by Joseph Simons that were performed at the college in later decades: *Zeno* in 1634, *Leo Armenus* (a.k.a. *Ultio divina*) in 1645, and *Mercia* in 1648, all of which survive in a number of different seventeenth-century printed and manuscript sources. Their author, an English priest born in Portsmouth, received his training at St. Omer's and the VEC before teaching in Liège and becoming rector of the VEC in 1647 and then rector of the theologate in Liège in 1650. Simons eventually returned to Britain as provincial for the English mission in the 1660s. He wrote numerous tragedies that were acted at the VEC, St. Omer's, and other Catholic colleges on the Continent.[178]

Zeno, Leo Armenus, and *Mercia* each tell a gruesome tale of a bloodthirsty ancient tyrant who ultimately receives his comeuppance, narratives valorizing the devout martyr archetype within heavily Orientalized imaginings of the distant past. *Mercia*'s antagonist is the medieval Pagan King Ulferus of British Mercia. In *Zeno* and *Leo Armenus*, these villains are two power-hungry Byzantine emperors who have renounced Eastern Christian Orthodoxy: the

---

[177] Rectangulum, Act II, Scene 6, Sutton (ed.), "The Jesuit Playlet *Blame Not Our Author*."
[178] T. Cooper and A. Shell, "Lobb, Emmanuel [*alias* Joseph Simons]" in *Oxford Dictionary of National Biography* (2004), https://doi.org/10.1093/ref:odnb/25561.

Isaurian emperor Zeno and Leo V the Armenian. Both stories end in brutal tyrannicide.[179] Although these three tragedies emphasize secular political drama over overtly confessional theatre, scholars such as Christopher Archibald, James Parente Jr., and Alison Shell have established that Simons's plotlines are barely camouflaged negative renderings of Protestant iconoclasm, the Anglican church, and Stuart absolutism, especially of the monarchy's predilection for opulent court entertainments. These plays resist equation of Catholicism with English Royalism. They were staged after a sharp rise in anti-Catholic sentiment and executions of priests in England. The Roman *argomento* for *Leo Armenus*, for instance, directly states that the tragedy was not far removed from recent events in England, and it harshly condemns English Protestant iconoclasm. By 1645 Henrietta Maria's Catholic chapel and the Canterbury Cathedral, dedicated to the college's patron saint, had both been ransacked and vandalized by iconoclasts.[180] Johnny Ignacio and Mark Chambers have also argued for a reading of *Leo Armenus* that considers how the drama's confessional politics intersect with its allusions to Jesuit evangelism in the East.[181] Additionally, these plays followed a trend in contemporary Barberini court opera to set musical martyr tragedies in Roman antiquity.[182] Byzantium and British Mercia offered parallel but more unique narrative contexts for exploring themes of ancient martyrdom.

In *Leo Armenus*, which was attended by the Cardinal Camillo Pamphili (brother of Pope Innocent X, Giovanni Battista Pamphili) and up to eleven other Roman cardinals, Leo the Armenian hosts a drunken musical dance and pantomime about Alexander the Great, at which Leo's leading general Michael Balbus is seized by the emperor's guards.[183] Pantomime dances in

---

[179] For extensive lists of early sources for these plays, see Oldani and Fischer (eds.), *Jesuit Theatre Englished*; Simons, *Leo Armenus, Mercia, sive Pietatis Coronata*, and *Zeno* in D. Sutton (ed.), *The Philological Museum* (see below); and Wiggins and Richardson, "2083. Mercia," "2345. Immanitate Zenonis [The Inhumanity of Zeno]" and "2247. Ultio divina [Divine Vengeance]" in *British Drama 1533–1642*, Vol. 8 (2017).

[180] See C. Archibald, "English Catholic Literary Culture, 1640–1660," unpublished D.Phil. diss., University of Oxford (2022), 67–88; J. A. Parente Jr., "Tyranny and Revolution on the Baroque Stage: The Dramas of Joseph Simons," *Humanistica Lovaniensia* 32 (1983): 309–24; and Shell, *Catholicism, Controversy and the English Literary Imagination, 1558–1660*, 207–10.

[181] J. Ignacio and M. Chambers, "Byzantines in English Jesuit Drama: Performing Joseph Simons's *Leo the Armenian*," in M. Öğütcü and A. Hussain (eds.), *Materializing the East in Early Modern English Drama* (London: Bloomsbury, 2023), 59–83.

[182] For Barberini operas and martyrs of ancient Rome, see Lamothe, "The Theater of Piety."

[183] Act III, Scenes 1–2, *Leo Armenus*, trans. P. C. Fischer in Oldani and Fischer (eds.), *Jesuit Theatre Englished*, 349–55; Wiggins and Richardson, "2247. Ultio divina [Divine Vengeance]." Archibald has discovered an early three-act manuscript version of the play that was used as the script for the VEC production. As I am unable to access the manuscript at this time, I have had to rely on the later 1656 printed script that has been translated. The musical scenes that I have referenced appear to all be included in the earlier manuscript version as well.

Roman musical theatre were closely associated with sin, for example in the 1635 Barberini opera *I Santi Didimo e Teodora*, in which the martyr Theodora watches a ballet of temptations that concludes with a martial dance.[184] This was common in English antimasques as well.[185] On the early modern stage, musical excess and discord were often attached to overconsumption of alcohol as indicators of poor physio-psychological health.[186] Just as the dodgy character Rectangulum is the one to sing a drinking song in *Comedy of Geometry*, the intoxicated party in *Leo Armenus* is not a martyr but the sinful emperor's court.

Balbus's grieving son Theophilus, who believes his father to have been murdered, drowns his own sorrows in the more solemn, subdued music of a singer-harpist named Philodus:

> The harp that once proclaimed our home happy must now sing of its misery. So be it. Let us weep over the fate of my slain father. Stay here with me, Philodus, loyal guardian of a home turned upside down. Take up the harp again and play it sadly. Mourn the death of Balbus with that splendid voice of yours.[187]

Theophilus adheres to English theatrical conventions of ventriloquized song, entreating a servant to sing a lament in his stead. In English drama it was typical for honorable male characters to also restrict their enjoyment of music to private contexts. Unlike the depraved Leo, Theophilus listens to music behind closed doors.[188] For the VEC's audiences, Philodus and his harp likely would have called to mind the holy psalmody of the ancient singer-harpist King David of Israel. Depictions of his music making pervaded Jesuit and other Roman dramatic spectacle of the time.[189]

Balbus, however, is in fact alive, and in the play's final act, Leo hears a series of ominous sounds portending his own demise, all of which harken back to the Classical imagery of Ovid and Virgil: the funereal hooting of an owl, the howl of a Tartarean dog, and the rumble of thunder.[190] All three nocturnal sounds were early modern theatrical proxies for mental disorder, divine justice, and dark premonition; usually, they were omens of imminent bloodshed. Audiences might have found this acousmatic offstage sound harrowing, as it invited

---

[184] Murata, *Operas for the Papal Court, 1631–1668*, 182, 254.
[185] Ravelhofer, *The Early Stuart Masque*, 67–71; Winkler, *O Let Us Howle Some Heavy Note*, 121–32.
[186] Winkler, *O Let Us Howle Some Heavy Note*.
[187] Theophilus, Act IV, Scene 3, *Leo Armenus*, trans. Fischer in Fischer in Oldani and Fischer (eds.), *Jesuit Theatre Englished*, 366–7.
[188] Wong, *Music and Gender in English Renaissance Drama*, 56–65.
[189] See Hammond, *Music & Spectacle in Baroque Rome*, 131–2, 185; and Lamothe, "The Theater of Piety," 51, 118.
[190] Act V, Scene 1, *Leo Armenus*, trans. Fischer in Oldani and Fischer (eds.), *Jesuit Theatre Englished*, 368–9.

spectator-auditors to construct any number of petrifying imaginings of its unlocatable source. Ringing bells, though usually a sonic indicator of Christian piety, could also allude to themes of divine judgment.[191]

On Christmas Day Leo is executed at the altar in the Hagia Sophia cathedral and Balbus usurps his throne, exclaiming, "From every side sweet music strikes my ears." This violent scene is accompanied by ringing bells (or, the emperor's death knell) and organ music, as well as psalmody, hymnody, and the Antiphon to the Magnificat for Christmas Matins:

PRIEST: [*as the organ falls silent*] Domine, labia, etc.
CHOIR: [*sings response from within, then sings:*] Christus natus est hodie, venite adoremus. [*At the end the emperor intones: "Christe, Redemptor omnium." The conspirators posing as canons attend him honoris causa, one on each side.*]
LEO: Christe, Redemptor omnium.
FIRST GUARD: You are the destroyer of everything [*He strikes the emperor, who seizes the cross from the high altar and vainly tries to defend himself.*] At long last you shall die.[192]

The real-life emperor Leo V (c. 775–820) was reputed to be an iconoclast burdened with both a hideous singing voice and a lack of self-awareness. He supposedly insisted upon intoning the chant in religious services, deluded into thinking that he was well suited for the job.[193] The true quality of his singing voice and the location of his actual assassination have long been debated.[194] By 1645 Hagia Sophia had been converted into a mosque with its belltower removed. Leo's organ-accompanied death in this setting might have appeared to spectator-auditors in Rome a condemnation of both Protestant iconoclasm and Islamic practices in the Ottoman Empire. In early modern English literary sources, the organ was repeatedly held up against other Levantine religio-cultural practices as an emblem of European Christian virtue.[195] Relatedly, the collapsing of anti-Protestant and anti-Islamic rhetoric is typical of early

---

[191] See Winkler, *O Let Us Howle Some Heavy Note*, and Wright, *Sound Effects*.
[192] Act V, Scenes 3–4, *Leo Armenus*, trans. Fischer in Oldani and Fischer (eds.), *Jesuit Theatre Englished*, 372–8.
[193] N. K. Moran, *Singers in Late Byzantine and Slavonic Painting* (Leiden: Brill, 1986), 51–8.
[194] See S. S. R. Frøyshov, "The Early History of the Hagiopolitan Daily Office in Constantinople," *Dumbarton Oaks Papers* 74 (2020): 351–82.
[195] S. Rettenbacher, "Hagia Sophia and the Third Space: An Enquiry into the Discursive Construction of Religious Sites," in U. Winkler, L. R. Fernández, and O. Leirvik (eds.), *Contested Spaces, Common Ground: Space and Power Structures in Contemporary Multireligious Societies* (Leiden: Brill, 2016), 105; and Wood, *Sounding Otherness in Early Modern Drama and Travel*, 99–148. For English musical drama and Constantinople, see also Ravelhofer, *The Early Stuart Masque*, 230–61.

modern VEC sermons, which paint the English Catholic cause as just one aspect of the Church's wider global campaign against the infidel.[196]

In *Zeno* and *Mercia*, the evil tyrants and their courtiers initially enjoy themselves at a hunt, at coronations, and at Bacchanal and military ballets, all to the sounds of horns, bugles, "rumbling drums," and "blaring" or "roaring" trumpets.[197] Both dramas are punctuated by constant musical *entr'actes*. The college's pantomime dances appear to have been influenced by the French *ballet de cour*, the *commedia dell'arte*, Jesuit ballet practices, and contemporary Roman opera.[198] One such ballet in *Zeno* calls for multiple women characters, an unusual occurrence in Jesuit drama: "Bacchus is accompanied in his chariot by his female attendants, who are making melody with voice and stringed instruments. Bacchus is leading the music." This scandalous dance is followed by a ballet performed by "seven black youths dressed in Turkish garb." They alternate their dancing with a ballet by four satyrs, after which Zeno remarks, "I like that ballet by Pluto's young men."[199] The ballet in so-called Turkish garb must have been a *moresca*, an older Italianate sword dance customarily performed in blackface.

Despite the many immoral connotations of satyr ballets and *moresche* in early modern theatre, both dances were a staple of Barberini and other Roman musical entertainments. In many cases, they were danced on-stage by explicitly demonic beings.[200] The *moresca* did occasionally come under fire in Counter-Reformation Rome for its deviant representations of the grotesque, viewed as antithetical to the values and aesthetics of the Church.[201] *Zeno*'s

---

[196] Underwood, "Representing England in Rome."

[197] Act I, Scene 1, Act III, Scenes 1–2, and Act V, Scenes 5–9, *Zeno*, trans. M. A. Haworth in Oldani and Fischer (eds.), *Jesuit Theatre Englished*, 5–6, 36–42, 66–72; Act I, Scenes 4–5 and Act II, Scenes 1–2, *Mercia*, trans. Grady in Oldani and Fischer (eds.), *Jesuit Theatre Englished*, 88–90, 94–100, 139–42. In Act II, Scene 1 of *Zeno*, the emperor's son Longinus harshly commands a lutenist to play for him and the two enter into a dialogue about Orphic music. This scene seems to have been omitted from the VEC production. Wiggins and Richardson, "2345. *Immanitate Zenonis* [The Inhumanity of Zeno]" and *Zeno*, trans. Haworth in Oldani and Fischer (eds.), *Jesuit Theatre Englished*, 20–1.

[198] For an overview of Simons's pantomime ballets, see McCabe, *An Introduction to Jesuit Theater*, 203–21.

[199] Act V, Scene 8, *Zeno*, trans. Haworth in Oldani and Fischer (eds.), *Jesuit Theatre Englished*, 68–71.

[200] Hammond, *Music & Spectacle in Baroque Rome*, 131–2, 192–8; Lamothe, "The Theater of Piety," 243–5; Murata, "*Dal ridicolo al diletto signorile*," 273.

[201] M. Kavvadia, "The *Moresca* Dance in Counter-Reformation Rome: Court Medicine and the Moderation of Exceptional Bodies," in M. Bondestam (ed.), *Exceptional Bodies in Early Modern Culture: Concepts of Monstrosity before the Advent of the Normal* (Amsterdam: Amsterdam University Press, 2020), 37–58. For other recent work on the *moresca* and Italianate blackface theatre in England, see R. Hornback, *Racism and Early Blackface Comic Traditions: From the Old World to the New* (Cham: Palgrave Macmillan, 2018); E. Jaffe-Berg, *Commedia dell'arte and the Mediterranean: Charting Journeys and Mapping "Others"* (Farnham: Ashgate, 2015); R. P. Locke, *Music and the Exotic from the Renaissance to Mozart* (Cambridge: Cambridge University Press, 2015), 165–80; M. Marrapodi (ed.), *The Routledge Research Companion to Anglo-Italian Renaissance Literature and Culture* (London: Routledge, 2019), https://doi.org/

exoticized, racialized representation of "Moorish" dancers imitating underworld beings is deployed to represent the emperor's barbarity, lasciviousness, and impending damnation. This scene identifies the VEC as one possible point of theatrical exchange that contributed to the popularization of Continental blackface practices in seventeenth-century English drama, at a historical moment in which England was developing foundational ideas of racial difference, establishing colonies throughout the world, and intensifying its aggressive participation in the Atlantic slave trade. The Society of Jesus, too, was deeply involved in the global slave trade and complicit in this racializing discourse.[202] *Zeno* was not the only VEC play to propagate such racializing tropes: A Moorish captain named Don Basilico in *The New Moon*, for instance, expresses his anger that the rays of Phoebus have burned his nation black. At one point in the play, Don Basilico is unjustly villainized when accused of murder.[203]

Mercia also finds its heretical characters at a musical procession honoring a host of "false" Greco-Roman gods, one of whom is Phoebus, after which the gods dance. This collection of heathen idols would have been more familiar to Roman audiences than the deities of ancient British paganism. Only the song's text survives, which praises the gods' more shallow and violent attributes: fame, riches, cunning, charisma, idolatrous shrines, physical strength, and skill in combat:

> THEORGUS: ... Jove will bring honors; Pluto, the wealth of Pergamum; Apollo, a name renowned; Mars, a spirit dismayed by evils; Hercules, strength
> [*At this point, there is a procession of false gods, each preceded by his own page. The pages celebrate the gods by singing songs about each one's gift.*]
>
> > Of gods and men the king is Jupiter,
> > Who claims the highest altars for himself.
> > The scepters of the world are his to give,
> > And royal trappings, too.

10.4324/9781315612720; M. Otter, "The Neapolitan *Moresche*: Impersonation and Othering," *Mediaevalia* 31 (2010): 143–69; Salvatore, "Parodie realistiche"; S. Schmalenberger, "Hearing Other in *The Masque of Blackness*," in N. André, K. M. Bryan, and E. Saylor (eds.), *Blackness in Opera* (Urbana: University of Illinois Press, 2012), 32–54; V. M. Vaughan, *Performing Blackness on English Stages, 1500–1800* (Cambridge: Cambridge University Press, 2005); E. Wilbourne, "'... la curiosità del personaggio': 'il Moro' on the Mid-Century Operatic Stage," in K. van Orden (ed.), *Seachanges: Music in the Mediterranean and Atlantic Worlds, 1550–1800* (Florence: Harvard University Press, 2021), 133–48, "*Lo Schiavetto* (1612)," and *Voice, Slavery, and Race in Seventeenth-Century Florence*; and Wilbourne and Cusick (eds.), *Acoustemologies in Contact*.

[202] For recent scholarship on Jesuits, race, and slavery, see N. Millett and C. H. Parker (eds.), *Jesuits and Race: A Global History of Continuity and Change, 1530–2020* (Albuquerque: University of New Mexico Press, 2022).

[203] Wiggins and Richardson, "2397. *The New Moon*."

Celebrity to dazzle all the earth,
Effulgence like the sun's, is Phoebus's gift
To those who worship him.
Their fame survives into eternity.

Progenitor of all the wars is Mars.
He lends his savage sword to ruthless men.
The boundless fury burning in his heart
Sets blazes everywhere.

A silver tongue! That comes from Mercury,
Whose suasive speeches silence other gods.
Great forcefulness of mind is in his gift,
And sparkling flow of words.

Great Hercules will generously bestow
Lithe mightiness of torso and of limb
And shoulders broad enough to bear the weight
Of all the skies above.

The opulence for which he is renowned
Will Pluto grant, rich veins of far-found gold
And king-beguiling worldly luxuries
And golden palaces.

And so, dear princes twain, to these six gods
Make offerings of incense from the East,
And drench their altar with the thick red blood
Of sacrificial lambs.[204]

The tide eventually turns for both tyrants. The inebriated Zeno is dethroned and buried alive at his own satyr dance, while the sons of Ulferus, Ufaldus and Ruffinus, are converted to Christianity before their father martyrs them and then himself converts. The ill fate of both regimes is foreshadowed, once again, by the predatory "screech owl."[205] When Zeno visits a magician-astrologer who predicts that the emperor will die a gruesome death, Zeno shouts,

> You owl with your ill-boding hoot. You are an echo from the land of the dead! Infernal Pluto's trumpet! You ominous screech owl! [*trying to choke the magician*] I'll strangle you so you'll spit out your tongue.[206]

---

[204] For brevity, I have only included English translations of these Latin songs in Simons's dramas. Act V, Scene 1, *Mercia*, trans. Oldani and Fischer (eds.), Grady in *Jesuit Theatre Englished*, 139–42.

[205] For the screech owl in early modern English drama, see Wright, *Sound Effects*, 73–114.

[206] Act I, Scene 2, *Zeno*, trans. Haworth in Oldani and Fischer (eds.), *Jesuit Theatre Englished*, 9.

In *Mercia* the evocation of the screech owl is continuously juxtaposed against a priest's caged songbird that comforts itself in its exile from the nest by praising God with sweet, skillful singing.[207] In Act IV, for instance, this priest, Tityrus, tells the Pagan brigand Chorebus, "I curse the shrieking of your voice" shortly after Chorebus himself has portentously exclaimed, "I quiver all over with horror. With prophetic voice the screech owl sings of flames and fire."[208] Tityrus then turns to his captive songbird and says adoringly,

> But you, you nice little consolation in my task, joy of the countryside, sweet singer of the woods, harmless little siren, glory of the airy tribe, and always pleasing praiser of your Maker, if I have carried you an exile from your family nest, carefully fed you, and not permitted you to be deprived of any of your primary feathers, remember that now and make return. [209]

In Act V Tityrus offers the bird as a gift to the imprisoned Ruffinus and attempts to baptize the prince. Ruffinus responds, "I see in it a living image of my lot. A prison keeps it locked up, and yet it relieves its exile with its skillful warbling. Then why should not I, in chains for the love of Christ, make my days joyful by singing?"[210]

The inferiority of both Pagan and secular musicking is made starkly apparent in both tragedies when stunning music bursts forth from the heavens. In Act IV, Scene 4 of *Zeno*, the soon-to-be martyred patrician Pelagius grows emboldened by a vision of two floating angels singing a hymn, followed by another heavenly piece sung by an offstage chorus. The first angel refers to Pelagius as a "mighty warrior" and "supreme champion," drawing on the language of Jesuit militarism. The first angel even goes so far as to suggest that the "fiery eloquence" of Pelagius's speaking voice has the power to disembowel his enemies.

> *While praying, PELAGIUS is in ecstasy and is strengthened by a heavenly vision. Above either side of the altar, by means of stage machinery, two angels can be seen as if poised in midair. They sing a hymn and then converse as follows.*

FIRST ANGEL: Mighty warrior, supreme champion. Heaven has heard your prayers ... Being a master of oratory, let the lofty towers echo with the thunder of your fiery eloquence. Your voice will churn up the very vitals of the tyrants and burst asunder the bowels of their being.

---

[207] Act I, Scene 2, and Act II, Scenes 5–6, *Zeno*, trans. Haworth in Oldani and Fischer (eds.), *Jesuit Theatre Englished*, 9, 30–1; Act III, Scene 2, Act IV, Scene 2, and Act V, Scene 2, *Mercia*, trans. Grady in Oldani and Fischer (eds.), *Jesuit Theatre Englished*, 111, 124–8, 142–6.

[208] Tityrus and Chorebus, Act IV, Scene 2, *Mercia*, trans. Grady in Oldani and Fischer (eds.), *Jesuit Theatre Englished*, 124–7.

[209] Tityrus, Act IV, Scene 2, *Mercia*, trans. Grady in Oldani and Fischer (eds.), *Jesuit Theatre Englished*, 127.

[210] Ruffinus, Act V, Scene 2, *Mercia*, trans. Grady in Oldani and Fischer (eds.), *Jesuit Theatre Englished*, 142.

SECOND ANGEL: Then you will be hauled before the dread tribunal on a criminal charge. Do not be afraid of anything. Go there without fear. Do not be afraid of anything. God will inspire you with strength ... Look up at the radiant dome of the sky. You will be transported there in a splendid triumph with the rich trophies won by your death. Let the chorus acclaim this omen with song.

The Chorus sings offstage. PELAGIUS *remains in ecstasy until he is seized and arrested.*[211]

Likewise, the two princes' religious fervor in *Mercia* is in Act I, Scene 3 inspired by a holy vision of Christ descending "in the midst of angelical choirs," who beckon to the princes in song and invite them to become knights for the Church:

> Young men,
> Renowned in your descent from kings of old,
> Dispel your misty sleepiness.
> Behold the Son of God the Father,
> God of the very Godhead born,
> Eternal Mind's eternal Splendor, Christ.
> Aglow with God's own light, He comes
> From heaven's citadel down to the earth.
> For all the tender youth
> Of would-be knights like you,
> He summons you around His royal banner,
> Calls you both: "Ufaldus, come,
> And you, Ruffinus, come!"

Ruffinus afterwards raves, "[A] beauty luminous with ethereal glory, a lovely choir of winged beings, and a heavenly song, sung by a godlike voice – all suggest divinity. Clearly a God has passed among us."[212]

All music performed in Simons's plays at the VEC is now lost. As in *Zeno*, a harpsichordist was enlisted for *Leo Armenus*, and a soprano and violinist received payment as well.[213] The college Pilgrim Book, which recorded visitors to the VEC, mentions that "six or seven musicians and singers" dined at the college throughout the run of *Mercia*.[214] The diegetic angelic and liturgical music in these plays was probably a combination of plainchant and polyphony,

---

[211] Act IV, Scene 4, *Zeno*, trans. Haworth in Oldani and Fischer (eds.), *Jesuit Theatre Englished*, 53–4.
[212] Angelical choirs, Act I, Scene 3, *Mercia*, trans. Grady in Oldani and Fischer (eds.), *Jesuit Theatre Englished*, 82–6.
[213] Gossett, "Drama in the English College, Rome, 1591–1660," 79–80; Wiggins and Richardson, "2345. *Immanitate Zenonis.*"
[214] " ... 6 vel. septem Musici aut Cantores ... " Gossett, "Drama in the English College, Rome, 1591–1660," 86–7.

perhaps even polychoral music. *Mercia*'s angel duo might have sung an Italianate *concertato* duet, as was the fashion in Rome.[215] While it remains unclear who exactly provided this music, it was probably the responsibility of either the VEC's own English student singers or the college chapel's salaried Italian vocal consort. The latter ensemble was directed by both Mazzocchi and the resident VEC organist Francesco Margarini.[216]

These scenes at the VEC were an opportunity for the college to position itself not only as a maker of wonders on par with the *meraviglie* of papal opera, but also as a legitimate urban space of Catholic worship and sacred musical excellence invoking transcendent musical divinity. Cloud illusionism was all the rage in seventeenth-century Roman art and theatre. In Roman operatic productions, cloud machinery and heavenly *tableaux* habitually appeared before despondent martyr protagonists to reassure them of their righteousness.[217] The VEC's Roman audiences might have recognized *tableaux* of singing angels as a familiar choice from Italian martyr operas, such as the 1631 Barberini opera Il Sant'Alessio, *I Santi Didimo e Teodora*, and the 1643 Barberini opera *Il Sant'Eustachio* by Mazzocchi.[218] The college's floating angels could have even been the same singers who played such analogous angelic roles in papal productions. The great irony of Gotardi's earlier praise of the VEC's beatific "English" angels in *Campianus* is that those performers might not have been English at all.

9 Conclusions

The New Moon may not be a tragedy, but like other surviving English College plays, it does deal with themes of death, loss, and persecution. We have seen that in the drama's Roman performance context, its rhetoric surrounding Cynthia's cause parallels other discourse about Catholic martyrdom. At the start of *The New Moon*, a pair of close friends, the hunter Meleager and the arts student Sylvanus, withhold their support from Cynthia, as Sylvanus is bothered by moonlight and Meleager is loyal to his friend. Cynthia's page Vertumnus, however, persuades Meleager to play dead to convince Sylvanus that his friend has been murdered by Don Basilico for failing to help the moon. Racked with guilt, the devastated Sylvanus attempts suicide but learns just in time that Meleager has not really perished. The two happily reunite and ally with

---

[215] For the popularity of the *concertato* style in Rome, see Filippi, "*Roma Sonora*," in Jones, Wisch, and Ditchfield (eds.), *A Companion to Early Modern Rome, 1492–1692*, 266–81.

[216] See Dixon, "Music in the Venerable English College in the Early Baroque" and Gossett, "Drama in the English College, Rome, 1591–1660," 76–80.

[217] A. Buccheri, *The Spectacle of Clouds, 1439–1650* (Farnham: Ashgate, 2014), 169–78.

[218] Murata, *Operas for the Papal Court, 1631–1668*, 19–23, 28–31, 45–7, 221–6, 253–7, 342–4. See also Hammond, *Music & Spectacle in Baroque Rome*, and Lamothe, "Theater of Piety."

Cynthia. Beneath this tragic subplot is a martyrological subtext in which the presumed death of one entity spurs the other into action for a shared cause. In Act I, Scene 3, Vertumnus describes the two friends as "the signe Gemini in the Zodiacke, two lutes in one case, two soules in one skinne, and two winges of one byrd, the one helpes not without the other."[219] It is only through Meleager's staged demise that his soul twin and fellow winged songster is finally moved to help the tearful, ill-treated moon. So, too, did the VEC perform dramatizations of English Catholic martyrdom, steeped in vibrant demonstrations of affinity with Italo-Catholic cultural values, to secure support for the English mission from the college's powerful patrons.

From the Jacobean age through the Caroline period and Revolution, the musical martyr's tale at the VEC continued to attract international crowds and acclaim. Even after the college's dramatic storytelling moved away from more heavy-handed narratives of anti-Catholic violence in Tudor and early Stuart England, the holy Italianate harmonies of the Catholic martyr archetype continued to triumph time and time again over the Othered sonic barbarity and frivolity of the righteous sufferer's cruel opponents. To tell and retell this story for several decades, the VEC theatre amalgamated a transcultural multiplicity of musical practitioners, repertoires, forms, styles, and instruments, propelling a specific projection of the "English nation" to the forefront of cultural spectacle in the epicenter of Catholic Christendom.

The English mission gradually retreated from its fierce crusade against the Reformation, but martyrological theatre remained valuable to the global mission of the society and to the development of English cosmopolitanism and national identity. The college's dramaturgical fixation on confessional violence gave rise to an illustrious English musico-theatrical institution that ultimately transcended the confessional divide, attracting Anglican spectator-auditors in Rome and elevating the history, politics, and culture of Protestant England onto a renowned international stage. The VEC's play production declined drastically from the 1640s, probably resulting from the 1644 death of Urban VIII, at which point the Barberini family was forced to flee the city and few musical dramas were produced under the rule of the new Pope Innocent X.[220] Little is known about the VEC theatre or its music after the mid-seventeenth century. If college productions continued after that point, existing scholarship has not accounted for it.

Many questions linger about musical activity at the college in the early seventeenth century, such as how the English repertoires discussed above

---

[219] Vertumnus, Act I, Scene 3, *The New Moon*, AVCAU Scrittura 35/2, f. 8r.
[220] Lamothe, "Theater of Piety," 3–4, 90–1.

made their way to Rome in the first place. British archives for Catholic family households might hold answers. Music aside, further research is needed on the college's theatre program in general: play titles for most VEC productions are still unknown, and a detailed, comprehensive reception history of music and theatre at the college remains unwritten. Scholarship on the VEC would also benefit from more extensive dialogue with current, developing research on musico-dramatic and martyrological traditions in other early modern English, Roman, and Jesuit religious institutions. Given its abundance of resident Catholic figureheads and patronage of progressive Italian musical developments, Rome, the heart of global Catholicism, was a uniquely significant location for the flourishing of English Jesuit musical theatre. Even so, it would be well worth systematically comparing, for example, the musical choices made in different productions of Simons's plays, which were first staged at other English colleges abroad before they were altered for performance at the VEC. *Mercia* was first staged at St. Omer's, *Leo Armenus* is also thought to have premiered at St. Omer's, and *Zeno* was initially presented at St. Omer's and the English College of Saint Gregory in Seville.[221] *Zeno* was later performed at least four times at the Seminario Romano in the 1650s–70s.[222]

This research contributes to a rapidly growing literature on early modern music and mobility that encourages transnational music histories unbounded by territory, geography, language, religion, or ethnicity. This study also endeavors to productively subvert historiographical fictions of Anglo-Italian musical encounter as a purely one-way street of Italian influence disconnected from wider global power structures. Seventeenth-century English musical theatre was not at all contained to Britain. If music scholars accept that madrigals, *intermedi*, and Jesuit drama were all key building blocks of early Italian opera, how might the VEC and its English repertoires fit into opera's traditionally Italian origin story? If Francesco Barberini was the VEC's cardinal protector and Virgilio Mazzocchi worked at the college while composing dramatic music for the Barberini court, what could be learned from efforts to detect traces of VEC theatrical practices in early Roman opera? How, then, might narratives about the birth of English opera and Restoration musical culture be complicated by research into earlier English proto-operatic musical activity in Catholic seminaries abroad?

Broadening out from questions that prioritize bilateral conceptions of Anglo-Italian musical exchange, this study of musical drama at the English College also invites scholars to consider the global instigators and repercussions of intra-European transcultural musical exchange and Counter-Reformation

---

[221] Wiggins and Richardson, "2083. *Mercia*," "2345. *Immanitate Zenonis* [The Inhumanity of Zeno]," "2247. *Ultio divina* [Divine Vengeance]."
[222] Jakovac, "Performance Culture at the English College in Rome, *c.* 1579–1660."

cultural politics, with an eye to wider histories of early modern cosmopolitanism, nation building, and empire. The staged political dynamics of European musical martyr dramas certainly did not play out in isolation from the global aspirations of the society and of British imperial agents. British interactions with Italo-Catholic musical culture were entwined with England's rise to an unprecedented level of geopolitical and commercial power in the early modern Mediterranean, a story that would continue long after the curtain had gone down on English Jesuit theatre in Rome.

Bibliography

Manuscript Sources

Archivum Venerabilis Collegii Anglorum de Urbe, Rome
  Libri 262, 309, 314, 321
  Scritture 33/3, 33/5, 35/1–2

Biblioteca Apostolica Vaticana, Vatican City
  MS Vaticani Latini 8263

British Library, London
  Additional Manuscript 15117
  Egerton Manuscript 2971

The National Archives, London
  State Papers 14/76, 85/4–5, 99/15

Printed Sources to 1800

Morley, Thomas. *The First Booke of Balletts to Five Voyces*. London: Thomas Este, 1595.

Wilbye, John. *The First Set of English Madrigals to 3. 4. 5. and 6. Voices*. London: Printed by Thomas Este, 1598.

——— *The Second Set of Madrigales to 3. 4. 5. and 6. Parts*. London: Printed by Thomas Este for John Browne, 1609.

Printed Sources from 1800

Adelman, Jeremy. "Mimesis and Rivalry: European Empires and Global Regimes." *Journal of Global History* 10, no. 1 (2015): 77–98.

Ahrendt, Rebekah. "The Diplomatic Viol." In *International Relations, Music and Diplomacy: Sounds and Voices on the International Stage*, 93–114, edited by Frédéric Ramel and Cécile Prévost-Thomas. Cham: Palgrave Macmillan, 2018.

Anderson, Susan L. *Echo and Meaning on Early Modern English Stages*. Cham: Palgrave Macmillan, 2018.

Archibald, Christopher. "Actors, Soldiers, and Jesuits in Post-Reformation England: Joseph Simons' 1648 Oration on Robert Persons and the Mission to England." *The Seventeenth Century* 40, no. 2 (2025): 249–95.

——— "English Catholic Literary Culture, 1640–1660." Unpublished D.Phil. diss., University of Oxford, 2022.

Austern, Linda Phyllis. "Anne Boleyn, Musician: A Romance across Centuries and Media." In *Authorizing Early Modern European Women from Biography to Biofiction*, 141–56, edited by James Fitzmaurice, Naomi J. Miller, and Sara Steen. Amsterdam: Amsterdam University Press, 2022.

Both from the Ears and Mind: Thinking about Music in Early Modern England. Chicago: University of Chicago Press, 2020.

"Nature, Culture, Myth, and the Musician in Early Modern England." *Journal of the American Musicological Society* 51, no. 1 (1998): 1–47.

Balme, Christopher B., Piermario Vescovo, and Daniele Vianello, eds. *Commedia dell'Arte in Context*. Cambridge: Cambridge University Press, 2018.

Barbieri, Patrizio. "The Roman Gut String-Makers 1550–1950." *Studi musicali* 35, no. 1 (2006): 3–127.

Bayne, Brandon. *Missions Begin with Blood: Suffering and Salvation in the Borderlands of New Spain*. New York: Fordham University Press, 2022.

Berti, Michaela, Émilie Corswarem, and Jorge Morales, eds. *Music and the Identity Process: The National Churches of Rome and Their Networks in the Early Modern Period*. Turnhout: Brepols, 2019.

Breidenbach, Michael D. *Our Dear-Bought Liberty: Catholics and Religious Toleration in Early America*. Cambridge, MA: Harvard University Press, 2021.

Brown, David. "Wilbye [Willoughbye], John." In *Grove Music Online, Oxford Music Online*, 2001. https://doi.org/10.1093/gmo/9781561592630.article.30302.

Bryan, John. "'*Full of Art*, and *Profundity*': The Five-Part Consort Pavan as a Medium for Sophisticated Musical Expression and Compositional Cross-Reference in Late Renaissance England." In *Networks of Music and Culture in the Late Sixteenth and Early Seventeenth Centuries*, 185–201, edited by David J. Smith, and Rachelle Taylor. London: Routledge, 2013.

Buccheri, Alessandra. *The Spectacle of Clouds, 1439–1650*. Farnham: Ashgate, 2014.

Cañeque, Alejandro. "Iberian Imperial Rivalries and the Missionary Conquest of Japan." In *The Routledge Hispanic Studies Companion to Early Modern Spanish Literature and Culture*, 47–60, edited by Rodrigo Cacho Casal and Caroline Egan. London: Routledge, 2022.

"In the Shadow of Francis Xavier: Martyrdom and Colonialism in the Jesuit Asian Missions." *Journal of Jesuit Studies* 9 (2022): 438–58.

Cichy, Andrew. "'Changing Their Tune': Sacred Music and the Recasting of English Post-Reformation Identity at St. Alban's College, Valladolid." In *Listening to Early Modern Catholicism: Perspectives from Musicology*,

173–86, edited by Daniele Filippi and Michael J. Noone. Leiden: Brill, 2017.

"'How Shall We Sing the Song of the Lord in a Strange Land?' English Catholic Music after the Reformation to 1700: A Study of Institutions in Continental Europe." Unpublished D.Phil. thesis, University of Oxford, 2013.

"Music, Meditation, and Martyrdom in a Seventeenth-Century English Seminary." *Music & Letters* 97, no. 2 (2016): 205–20.

"Scheming Jesuits and Sound Doctrine?: The Influence of the Jesuits on English Catholic Music at Home and Abroad, c.1580–1640." In *Jesuit Intellectual and Physical Exchange between England and Mainland Europe, c. 1580–1789: "The World is Our House"?* 133–51, edited by James E. Kelly and Hannah Thomas. Leiden: Brill, 2019.

Clark, Alice V. "Carissimi's *Jephte* and Jesuit Spirituality." *College Music Symposium* 59, no. 1 (2019): 1–33.

Cooper, Thompson, and Alison Shell. "Lobb, Emmanuel [alias Joseph Simons]." In *Oxford Dictionary of National Biography*, 2004. https://doi.org/10.1093/ref:odnb/25561.

Corens, Liesbeth. *Confessional Mobility and English Catholics in Counter-Reformation Europe*. Oxford: Oxford University Press, 2019.

Curran, Robert Emmett. *Papist Devils: Catholics in British America, 1574–1783*. Washington, DC: The Catholic University of America Press, 2014.

de Carvalho, Francismar Alex Lopes. *Missionizing on the Edge: Religion and Power in the Jesuit Missions of Spanish Amazonia*. Leiden: Brill, 2023.

de Kisch, Marie-Anne. "A propos de Huit Pièces Inédites (1612–1614) dans les Archives du Collège Anglais de Rome." *Études Anglaises, Grande Bretagne-Ètats-Unis* 25 (1972): 525–9.

"Fêtes et représentations au Collège Anglais de Rome 1612–1614." In *Les Fêtes de la Renaissance*, 525–43, edited by Jean Jacquot and Elie Konigson. Paris: Editions du Centre national de la recherche scientifique, 1975.

de Lucca, Valeria. "Patronage." In *The Oxford Handbook of Opera*, 648–65, edited by Helen M. Greenwald. Oxford: Oxford University Press, 2014.

The Politics of Princely Entertainment: Music and Spectacle in the Lives of Lorenzo Onofrio and Maria Mancini Colonna. Oxford: Oxford University Press, 2020.

de Lucca, Valeria, and Christine Jeanneret, eds. *The Grand Theater of the World: Music, Space, and the Performance of Identity in Early Modern Rome*. London: Routledge, 2019.

del Amo Iribarren, Patxi Xabier. "Anthony Poole (c.1629–1692), the Viol and Exiled English Catholics." Unpublished Ph.D. diss., University of Leeds, 2011.

Dillon, Anne. *The Construction of Martyrdom in the English Catholic Community, 1535–1603*. London: Routledge, 2002.

Dixon, Graham. "Music in the Venerable English College in the Early Baroque." In *La musica a Roma attraverso le fonti d'archivio: Atti del Convegno internazionale Roma 4–7 giugno 1992*, 469–78, edited by Bianca Maria Antolini, Arnaldo Morelli, and Vera Vita Spagnuolo. Lucca: Libreria Musicale Italiana, 1994.

Duffin, Ross W. "Framing a Ditty for Elizabeth: Thoughts on Music for the 1602 Summer Progress." *Early Music History* 2020, no. 39 (2020): 115–48.

———. *Some Other Note: The Lost Songs of English Renaissance Comedy*. Oxford: Oxford University Press, 2018.

Flynn, Jane. "English Jesuit Missionaries, Music Education, and the Musical Participation of Women in Devotional Life in Recusant Households from ca. 1580–1630." In *Beyond Boundaries: Rethinking Music Circulation in Early Modern England*, 29–41, edited by Linda Phyllis Austern, Candace Bailey, and Amanda Eubanks Winkler. Bloomington: Indiana University Press, 2017.

Foley, Henry. *Records of the English Province of the Society of Jesus*. Vol. 7. London: Burns and Oates, 1882.

Frøyshov, Stig Simeon R. "The Early History of the Hagiopolitan Daily Office in Constantinople." *Dumbarton Oaks Papers* 74 (2020): 351–82.

Fuchs, Barbara. *Mimesis and Empire: The New World, Islam, and European Identities*. Cambridge: Cambridge University Press, 2001.

Fuchs, Barbara, and Emily Weissbourd, eds. *Representing Imperial Rivalry in the Early Modern Mediterranean*. Toronto: University of Toronto Press, 2015.

Fusaro, Maria. *Political Economies of Empire in the Early Modern Mediterranean: The Decline of Venice and the Rise of England, 1450–1700*. Cambridge: Cambridge University Press, 2015.

Games, Alison. *The Web of Empire: English Cosmopolitans in an Age of Expansion, 1560–1660*. Oxford: Oxford University Press, 2008.

Gibson, Jonathan. "Hearing the Viola da Gamba in 'Komm, süsses Kreuz'." In *Fiori musicali: Liber amicorum Alexander Silbiger*, 419–50, edited by Claire Fontijn and Susan Parisi. Sterling Heights: Harmonie Park Press, 2010.

Gollar, C. Walker. *"Let Us Go Free": Slavery and Jesuit Universities in America*. Washington, DC: Georgetown University Press, 2024.
Gossett, Suzanne, ed. "*Blame Not Our Author*, from the MS (Scrittura 35.1) at the Venerable English College, Rome." *Malone Society Collections* 2 (1983): 85–132.
——. "Drama in the English College, Rome, 1591–1660." *English Literary Renaissance* 3, no. 1 (1973): 60–93.
——. "English Plays in the English College Archives." *The Venerabile* 28, no. 1 (1983): 23–33.
Gouk, Penelope. "Music and Spirit in Early Modern Thought." In *Emotions and Health, 1200–1700*, 221–39, edited by Elena Carrera. Leiden: Brill, 2013.
Goulet, Anne-Madeleine, José María Dominguez, and Èlodie Oriel, eds. *Spectacles et performances artistiques à Rome (1644–1740): Une analyse historique à partir des archives familiales de l'aristocratie*. Rome: Publications de l'École française de Rome, 2021. https://doi.org/10.4000/books.efr.16344.
Grendler, Paul F. *Jesuit Schools and Universities in Europe, 1548–1773*. Leiden: Brill, 2018.
Hammond, Frederick. *Music & Spectacle in Baroque Rome: Barberini Patronage under Urban VIII*. New Haven: Yale University Press, 1994.
Hornback, Robert. *Racism and Early Blackface Comic Traditions: From the Old World to the New*. Cham: Palgrave Macmillan, 2018.
Ignacio, Johnny, and Mark Chambers. "Byzantines in English Jesuit Drama: Performing Joseph Simons's *Leo the Armenian*." In *Materializing the East in Early Modern English Drama*, 59–83, edited by Murat Öğütcü and Aisha Hussain. London: Bloomsbury, 2023.
Irving, David R. M. "Music in Global Jesuit Missions, 1540–1773." In *The Oxford Handbook of the Jesuits*, 598–634, edited by Ines G. Županov. New York: Oxford University Press, 2019.
Jaffe-Berg, Erith. *Commedia dell'arte and the Mediterranean: Charting Journeys and Mapping "Others."* Farnham: Ashgate, 2015.
Jakovac, Gašper. "Performance Culture at the English College in Rome, c. 1579–1660." In *The English Community of Rome, 1500–1829*, edited by Matteo Binasco. Brill, forthcoming in 2025.
Jones, Pamela M., Barbara Wisch, and Simon Ditchfields, eds. *A Companion to Early Modern Rome, 1492–1692*. Leiden: Brill, 2019.
Kavvadia, Maria. "The *Moresca* Dance in Counter-Reformation Rome: Court Medicine and the Moderation of Exceptional Bodies." In *Exceptional Bodies in Early Modern Culture: Concepts of Monstrosity before the*

Advent of the Normal, 37–58, edited by Maja Bondestam. Amsterdam: Amsterdam University Press, 2020.

Keener, Andrew S. "Japan Dramas and Shakespeare at St. Omers English Jesuit College." *Renaissance Quarterly* 74 (2021): 876–917.

Kendrick, Robert L. "Martyrdom in Seventeenth-Century Italian Music." In *From Rome to Eternity: Catholicism and the Arts in Italy, ca. 1550–1650*, 121–41, edited by Pamela M. Jones and Thomas Worcester. Leiden: Brill, 2002.

Kenny, Anthony, ed. *The Responsa Scholarum of the English College, Rome*. Vol. 2. Newport: The Catholic Record Society, 1963.

Kimbell, David. *Italian Opera*. Cambridge: Cambridge University Press, 1991.

Kirk, Stephanie. "Relics, Jesuit Masculinity, and the Performance of Martyrdom in *Triumpho de los Sanctos*." *Latin American Theatre Review* 54, no. 1 (2020): 79–98.

Körndle, Franz. "Between Stage and Divine Service: Jesuits and Theatrical Music." In *Music and the Renaissance: Renaissance, Reformation and Counter-Reformation*, 479–97, edited by Philippe Vendrix. London: Routledge, 2011.

Lamothe, Virginia Christy. "The Theater of Piety: Sacred Operas for the Barberini Family (Rome, 1632–1643)." Unpublished Ph.D. diss., University of North Carolina at Chapel Hill, 2009.

Lazarus, Micha. "Birdsongs and Sonnets: Acoustic Imitation in Renaissance Lyric." *Huntington Library Quarterly* 84, no. 4 (2021): 681–715.

Leech, Peter, and Maurice Whitehead. "'Clamores omnino atque admirationes excitant': New Light on Music and Musicians at St Omers English Jesuit College, 1658–1714." *Tijdschrift van de Koninklijke Vereniging voor Nederlandse Muziekgeschiedenis* 66, no. 1 (2016): 123–48.

———. "'In Paradise and among Angels': Music and Musicians at St. Omers English Jesuit College, 1593–1721." *Tijdschrift van de Koninklijke Vereniging voor Nederlandse Muziekgeschiedenis* 61, no. 1 (2011): 57–82.

Leopold, Silke. "Rome: Sacred and Secular." In *The Early Baroque Era: From the Late 16th Century to the 1660s*, 49–74, edited by Curtis Price. Basingstoke: Macmillan, 1993.

Locke, Ralph P. *Music and the Exotic from the Renaissance to Mozart*. Cambridge: Cambridge University Press, 2015.

Lockey, Brian. *Early Modern Catholics, Royalists, and Cosmopolitans: English Transnationalism and the Christian Commonwealth*. London: Routledge, 2016.

Long, Megan Kaes. "Characteristic Tonality in the *Balletti* of Gastoldi, Morley, and Hassler." *Journal of Music Theory* 59, no. 2 (2015): 235–71.

Hearing Homophony: Tonal Expectation at the Turn of the Seventeenth Century. Oxford: Oxford University Press, 2020.
Ludwig, Loren. "'Equal to All Alike': A Cultural History of the Viol Consort in England, c. 1550–1675." Unpublished Ph.D. diss., University of Virginia, 2011.
Lyon, Elizabeth L. "'Magis corde quam organo': Agazzari, Amadino, and the Hidden Meanings of *Eumelio*." *Early Music* 48, no. 2 (2020): 156–76.
MacNeil, Anne E. "Celestial Sirens of the Commedia dell'Arte Stage." In *The Routledge Companion to the Commedia dell'Arte*, 246–54, edited by Judith Chaffee and Olly Crick. London: Routledge, 2015.
Mahaffy, Caitlin. "'Melodious Madrigals': A Study of Animal Musicians in Early Modern England." *The Ben Jonson Journal* 27, no. 1 (2020): 126–43.
Mailes, Alana. "Singing Nuns and Soft Power: British Diplomats as Music Tourists in Seicento Venice." *Religions* 13, no. 4 (2022): 330–44.
Mailes, Alana, and Maurice Whitehead. "A Stuart Musician's Conversion to Catholicism: Richard Dering and the Venerable English College, Rome." *Music & Letters* 106, no. 1 (2025): 1–28.
Marrapodi, Michele, ed. *The Routledge Research Companion to Anglo-Italian Renaissance Literature and Culture.* London: Routledge, 2019. https://doi.org/10.4324/9781315612720.
Marsh, Christopher. *Music and Society in Early Modern England.* Cambridge: Cambridge University Press, 2010.
Masur, Laura E. "Plantation as Mission: American Indians, Enslaved Africans, and Jesuit Missionaries in Maryland." *Journal of Jesuit Studies* 8 (2021): 385–407.
Mazzio, Carla. "The Three-Dimensional Self: Geometry, Melancholy, Drama." In *Arts of Calculation: Quantifying Thought in Early Modern Europe*, 39–65, edited by David Glimp and Michelle R. Warren. New York: Palgrave Macmillan, 2004.
McCabe, William H. *An Introduction to the Jesuit Theater: A Posthumous Work*, edited by Louis J. Oldani. Saint Louis: Institute of Jesuit Sources, 1983.
―――. "Music and Dance on a 17th-Century College Stage." *The Musical Quarterly* 24, no. 3 (1938): 313–22.
McCoog, Thomas M. "'The Slightest Suspicion of Avarice': The Finances of the English Jesuit Mission." *Recusant History* 19, no. 2 (1988): 103–23.
Medić, Milena. "From Pain to Pleasure: The Troping of Elegy in the Renaissance Italian Madrigal." *Muzikologija* 1, no. 22 (2017): 151–75.

Millett, Nathaniel, and Charles H. Parker, eds. *Jesuits and Race: A Global History of Continuity and Change, 1530–2020*. Albuquerque: University of New Mexico Press, 2022.

Miola, Robert S. "Jesuit Drama in Early Modern England." In *Theatre and Religion: Lancastrian Shakespeare*, 71–86, edited by Richard Dutton, Alison Findlay, and Richard Wilson. Manchester: Manchester University Press, 2003.

Moran, Neil K. *Singers in Late Byzantine and Slavonic Painting*. Leiden: Brill, 1986.

Murata, Margaret. "Allegorical Figures and Music in Seventeenth-Century Spanish and Italian Scripts." In *La Comedia nueva e le scene italiane nel Seicento: Trame, drammaturgie, contesti a confronto*, 177–97, edited by Fausta Antonucci and Anna Tedesco. Florence: Leo S. Olschki, 2016.

"Barberini." In *Grove Music Online, Oxford Music Online*, 2001. https://doi.org/10.1093/gmo/9781561592630.article.01998.

"*Dal ridicolo al diletto signorile*: Rospigliosi and the Intermedio in Rome." In *La Musique à Rome au xviie siècle: Études et perspectives de recherche*, 269–89, edited by Caroline Giron-Panel and Anne-Madeleine Goulet. Rome: Publications de l'École française de Rome, 2012.

"Opera as Spectacle, Opera as Drama." In *The Cambridge Companion to Seventeenth-Century Opera*, 77–101, edited by Jacqueline Weber. Cambridge: Cambridge University Press, 2021.

Operas for the Papal Court, 1631–1668. Ann Arbor: UMI Research Press, 1981.

"The Recitative Soliloquy." *Journal of the American Musicological Society* 32, no. 1 (1979): 45–73.

"*Theatri intra theatrum* or, the Church and the Stage in Seventeenth-Century Rome." In *Sleuthing the Muse: Essays in Honor of William Prizer*, 181–200, edited by Kristine K. Forney. New York: Pendragon Press, 2012.

Murphy, Emilie K. M. "A Sense of Place: Hearing English Catholicism in the Spanish Habsburg Territories, 1568–1659." In *Sensing the Sacred in Medieval and Early Modern Culture*, 136–57, edited by Robin MacDonald, Emilie K. M. Murphy, and Elizabeth L. Swann. London: Routledge, 2018.

"Music and Catholic Culture in Post-Reformation Lancashire: Piety, Protest, and Conversion." *British Catholic History* 32, no. 4 (2015): 492–525.

"Music and Post-Reformation English Catholics: Place, Sociability, and Space, 1570–1640." Unpublished Ph.D. diss., University of York, 2014.

"Musical Self-Fashioning and the 'Theatre of Death' in Late Elizabethan and Jacobean England." *Renaissance Studies* 30, no. 3 (2015): 410–29.

Murray, Tessa. *Thomas Morley: Elizabethan Music Publisher.* Woodbridge: Boydell Press, 2014.

Nasifoglu, Yelda. "Embodied Geometry in Early Modern Theatre." In *The Best Writing on Mathematics 2021*, 77–81, edited by Mircea Pitici. Princeton: Princeton University Press, 2022.

Netzloff, Mark. "The English Colleges and the English Nation: Allen, Persons, Verstegan, and Diasporic Nationalism." In *Catholic Culture in Early Modern England*, 236–60, edited by Ronald Corthell, Frances Dolan, Christopher Highley, and Arthur F. Marotti. Indiana: University of Notre Dame Press, 2007.

Nicholson, Eric. "Crossing Borders with Satyrs, the Irrepressible Genre-Benders of Pastoral Tragicomedy." *The Italianist* 40, no. 3 (2020): 342–61.

Norland, Howard B. "Neo-Latin Drama in Britain." In *Neo-Latin Drama and Theatre in Early Modern Europe*, 471–544, edited by Jan Bloemendal and Norland. Leiden: Brill, 2013.

"Political Martyrdom at the English College in Rome." In *Politics and Aesthetics in European Baroque and Classicist Tragedy*, 135–51, edited by Jan Bloemendal and Nigel Smith. Leiden: Brill, 2016.

O'Donnell, Catherine. *Jesuits in the North American Colonies and the United States: Faith, Conflict, Adaptation.* Leiden: Brill, 2020.

Oba, Haruka, Akihiko Watanabe, and Florian Schaffenrath, eds. *Japan on the Jesuit Stage: Transmissions, Receptions, and Regional Contexts.* Leiden: Brill, 2022.

Oldani, Louis J., and Philip C. Fischer, eds. *Jesuit Theatre Englished: Five Tragedies of Joseph Simons.* St. Louis: The Institute of Jesuit Sources, 1989.

Oldani, Louis J., and Victor R. Yanitelli. "Jesuit Theater in Italy: Its Entrances and Exit." *Italica* 76, no. 1 (1999): 18–32.

Otter, Monika. "The Neapolitan *Moresche*: Impersonation and Othering." *Mediaevalia* 31 (2010): 143–69.

Otterstedt, Annette. *The Viol: History of an Instrument.* Kassel: Bärenreiter, 2002.

Parente, James A. Jr. "Tyranny and Revolution on the Baroque Stage: The Dramas of Joseph Simons." *Humanistica Lovaniensia* 32 (1983): 309–24.

Pike, Lionel. *Pills to Purge Melancholy: The Evolution of the English Ballett.* Aldershot: Ashgate, 2004.

Piperno, Franco. "Cardinals, Music, and Theatre." In *A Companion to the Early Modern Cardinal*, 600–15, edited by Mary Hollingsworth, Miles Pattenden, and Arnold Witte. Leiden: Brill, 2020.

Ravelhofer, Barbara. *The Early Stuart Masque: Dance, Costume and Music*. Oxford: Oxford University Press, 2006.

Rettenbacher, Sigrid. "Hagia Sophia and the Third Space: An Enquiry into the Discursive Construction of Religious Sites." In *Contested Spaces, Common Ground: Space and Power Structures in Contemporary Multireligious Societies*, 95–112, edited by Ulrich Winkler, Lidia Rodríguez Fernández, and Oddbjørn Leirvik. Leiden: Brill, 2016.

Reynolds, Matthew. *Godly Reformers and their Opponents in Early Modern England: Religion in Norwich, c.1560–1643*. Woodbridge: Boydell and Brewer, 2005.

Richardson, Carol M. "Durante Alberti, the *Martyrs' Picture* and the Venerable English College, Rome." *Papers of the British School at Rome* 73 (2005): 223–63.

Roque, Ricardo. "Mimesis and Colonialism: Emerging Perspectives on a Shared History." *History Compass* 13, no. 4 (2015): 201–11.

Rosand, Ellen. "The Descending Tetrachord: An Emblem of Lament." *The Musical Quarterly* 65, no. 3 (1979): 346–59.

———. "Monteverdi's Mimetic Art: *L'Incoronazione di Poppea*." *Cambridge Opera Journal* 1, no. 2 (1989): 113–37.

———. *Opera in Seventeenth-Century Venice: The Creation of a Genre*. Berkeley: University of California Press, 1991.

Salvatore, Gianfranco. "Parodie realistiche: Africanismi, fraternità e sentimenti identitari nelle canzoni moresche del Cinquecento." *Kronos* 14 (2012): 97–130.

Santarelli, Cristina. *La gara degli elementi: acqua, aria, terra, e fuoco nelle feste sabaude (1585–1699)*. Lucca: Libreria Musicale Italiana, 2010.

Saulini, Mirella. "Twenty-Five Years of Research on Jesuit Drama: An Italian Contribution to the History of Theatre." In *Új eredmények a színház- és drámatörténeti kutatásban (17–19. század): Tanulmányok a dráma- és színháztörténet köréből*, 145–54, edited by Anett Farkas and Gabriella Körömi. Eger: Eszterházy Károly Katolikus Egyetem Líceum Kiadó, 2022.

Schmalenberger, Sarah. "Hearing Other in *The Masque of Blackness*." In *Blackness in Opera*, 32–54, edited by Naomi André, Karen M. Bryan, and Eric Saylor. Urbana: University of Illinois Press, 2012.

"Sellinger's Round [1]." *Traditional Tune Archive*. Updated August 7, 2020. https://tunearch.org/wiki/Annotation:Sellinger%27s_Round_(1).

Shell, Alison. "Autodidacticism in English Jesuit Drama: The Writings and Career of Joseph Simons." *Medieval & Renaissance Drama in England* 13 (2001): 34–56.

——. *Catholicism, Controversy and the English Literary Imagination, 1558–1660*. Cambridge: Cambridge University Press, 2004.

Simons, Joseph. *Leo Armenus* (1645), edited by Dana Sutton. *The Philological Museum*. Updated November 5, 2013. https://philological.cal.bham.ac.uk/leo/.

——. *Mercia, sive Pietatis Coronata* (1648), edited by Dana Sutton. *The Philological Museum*. Updated April 19, 2021. https://philological.cal.bham.ac.uk/mercia/.

——. *Zeno* (1645), edited by Dana Sutton. *The Philological Museum*. Updated January 10, 2014. https://philological.cal.bham.ac.uk/zeno/.

Spohr, Arne. "Concealed Music in Early Modern Diplomatic Ceremonial." In *Music and Diplomacy from the Early Modern Era to the Present*, 19–43, edited by Rebekah Ahrendt, Mark Ferraguto, and Damien Mahiet. New York: Palgrave Macmillan, 2014.

Spring, Matthew. *The Lute in Britain: A History of the Instrument and its Music*. Oxford: Oxford University Press, 2001.

Stilwell, Kenneth. "Adopting Rituals: The Jesuits and the Huron Noël, 'Jesous Ahatonnia'." In *Music as Cultural Mission: Explorations of Jesuit Practices in Italy and North America*, 143–61, edited by Anna Harwell Celenza and Anthony R. DelDonna. Philadelphia: Saint Joseph's University Press, 2014.

Sutto, Antoinette. *Loyal Protestants & Dangerous Papists: Maryland and the Politics of Religion in the English Atlantic, 1630–1690*. Virginia: University of Virginia Press, 2015.

Sutton, Dana. "English Jesuit Drama in the Sixteenth and Seventeenth Centuries." *Oxford Handbooks*, 2013. https://doi.org/10.1093/oxfordhb/9780199935338.013.003.

——, ed. "The Anonymous Tragedy *Roffensis*." *The Philological Museum*. Updated February 27, 2013. https://philological.cal.bham.ac.uk/roff/.

——, ed. "The Anonymous Tragedy *Thomas Cantuariensis* (1613)." *The Philological Museum*. Updated October 12, 2004. https://philological.cal.bham.ac.uk/thomcant/.

——, ed. "The Anonymous Tragedy *Thomas Morus* (1612)." *The Philological Museum*. Updated May 24, 2005. https://philological.cal.bham.ac.uk/more/.

ed. "The Anonymous Tragicomedy *Captiva Religio* (1614)." *The Philological Museum*. Updated August 12, 2006. https://philological.cal.bham.ac.uk/capt/.

ed. "The Intermedium *Minutum* (1613)." *The Philological Museum*. Updated August 2, 2006. https://philological.cal.bham.ac.uk/minutum?/.

ed. "The Jesuit Playlet *Blame Not Our Author.*" *The Philological Museum*. Updated November 2, 2021. https://philological.cal.bham.ac.uk/blamenot/.

Takao, Makoto Harris. "In What Storms of Blood from Christ's Flock is Japan Swimming?: Gratia Hosokawa and the Performative Representation of Japanese Martyrdom in *Mulier fortis* (1698)." In *Changing Hearts: Performing Jesuit Emotions between Europe, Asia, and the Americas*, 87–120, edited by Yasmin Haskell and Raphaële Garrod. Leiden: Brill, 2019.

Taylor, Rachelle. "Peter Philips (1560/1561–1628) and the Venerable English College, Rome." In *The Di Martinelli Music Collection (KULeuven, University Archives): Musical Life in Collegiate Churches in the Low Countries and Europe: Chant and Polyphony*, 243–60, edited by Bruno Bouckaert and Eugeen Schreurs. Leuven: Alamire, 2000.

Teo, Kian-Seng. "John Wilbye's Second Set of Madrigals (1609) and the Influence of Marenzio and Monteverdi." *Studies in Music* 20 (1986): 1–11.

Toft, Robert. *With Passionate Voice: Re-creative Singing in Sixteenth-Century England and Italy*. Oxford: Oxford University Press, 2014. https://doi.org/10.1093/ml/gcv120.

Treadwell, Nina. *Music and Wonder at the Medici Court: The 1589 Interludes for* La Pellegrina. Bloomington: Indiana University Press, 2008.

"Music of the Gods: Solo Song and *effetti meravigliosi* in the Interludes for *La pellegrina*." *Current Musicology* 83 (2007): 33–84.

Underwood, Lucy. "Representing England in Rome: Sermons from the Early Modern English College to Popes and Cardinals." *Reformation & Renaissance Review* 23 (2021): 4–26.

Ungerer, Gustav. "The Viol da Gamba as a Sexual Metaphor in Elizabethan Music and Literature." *Renaissance and Reformation* 8, no. 2 (1984): 79–80.

van Orden, Kate. "Music as a Sonic Record." *Huntington Library Quarterly* 82, no. 1 (2019): 17–42.

Music, Discipline, and Arms in Early Modern France. Chicago: University of Chicago Press, 2005.

Varwig, Bettina. *Music in the Flesh: An Early Modern Musical Physiology*. Chicago: University of Chicago Press, 2023.

Vaughan, Virginia Mason. *Performing Blackness on English Stages, 1500–1800*. Cambridge: Cambridge University Press, 2005.

Ward, John. "Music for *A Handefull of Pleasant Delites*." *Journal of the American Musicological Society* 10, no. 3 (1957): 151–80.

Wardhaugh, Benjamin. *Encounters with Euclid: How an Ancient Greek Geometry Text Shaped the World*. Princeton: Princeton University Press, 2021.

Wendland, John. "'Madre non mi far Monaca': The Biography of a Renaissance Folksong." *Acta Musicologica* 48, no. 2 (1976): 185–204.

Wiggins, Martin, and Catherine Richardson. *British Drama 1533–1642: A Catalogue*. Vols. 5–9. Oxford: Oxford University Press, 2015–18. https://doi.org/10.1093/actrade/9780198739111.book.1.

Wilbourne, Emily. "' ... la curiosità del personaggio': 'il Moro' on the Mid-Century Operatic Stage." In *Seachanges: Music in the Mediterranean and Atlantic Worlds, 1550–1800*, 133–48, edited by Kate van Orden. Florence: Harvard University Press, 2021.

———. "*Lo Schiavetto* (1612): Travestied Sound, Ethnic Performance, and the Eloquence of the Body." *Journal of the American Musicological Society* 63, no. 1 (2010): 1–44.

———. "Music, Race, Representation: Three Scenes of Performance at the Medici Court (1608–16)." *Il saggiatore musicale* 27, no. 1 (2020): 5–168.

———. *Seventeenth-Century Opera and the Sound of the Commedia dell'Arte*. Chicago: University of Chicago Press, 2016.

———. *Voice, Slavery, and Race in Seventeenth-Century Florence*. Oxford: Oxford University Press, 2023.

Wilbourne, Emily, and Suzanne G. Cusick, eds. *Acoustemologies in Contact: Sounding Subjects and Modes of Listening in Early Modernity*. Cambridge: Open Book, 2021.

Williams, Michael E. *The Venerable English College, Rome: A History*. Leominster: Gracewing, 2008.

Williams, Richard L. "Ancient Bodies and Contested Identities in the English College Martyrdom Cycle, Rome." In *Roman Bodies: Antiquity to the Eighteenth Century*, 185–200, edited by Andrew Hopkins and Maria Wyke. London: The British School at Rome, 2005.

Wilson, Christopher R. *Shakespeare's Musical Imagery*. London: Bloomsbury, 2015.

Winkler, Amanda Eubanks. *O Let Us Howle Some Heavy Note: Music for Witches, the Melancholic, and the Mad on the Seventeenth-Century English Stage*. Bloomington: Indiana University Press, 2006.

Wong, Katrine K. *Music and Gender in English Renaissance Drama*. London: Routledge, 2013.

Wood, Jennifer Linhart. *Sounding Otherness in Early Modern Drama and Travel: Uncanny Vibrations in the English Archive*. Cham: Palgrave Macmillan, 2019.

Woodfield, Ian. *The Early History of the Viol*. Cambridge: Cambridge University Press, 1984.

Wright, Laura Jayne. *Sound Effects: Hearing the Early Modern Stage*. Manchester: Manchester University Press, 2023.

Acknowledgments

Thank you to Kate van Orden, Emily Dolan, Kay Kaufman Shelemay, and Diego Pirillo for supervising this research. I am also grateful to Ross Duffin, Adam Gilbert, Rotem Gilbert, Iain Fenlon, Gašper Jakovac, Mary Laven, Dana Sutton, Maurice Whitehead, Martin Wiggins, and other colleagues at the University of Southern California, the University of Cambridge, Harvard University, Villa I Tatti, the Sapienza University of Rome, the American Academy in Rome, and the Venerable English College, Rome, for sharing their insights. Many thanks especially to Gašper, Kate, Maurice, Jen-yen Chen, Grace Edgar, Peter Elliott, Alan Howard, Heather Inwood, Lewis Morrin, and Bettina Varwig for reading drafts of this work. Thank you also to Michael Ennis, Sarah Koval, Claudia Terribile, and Rebecca Villarreal for their translation assistance. Many thanks also to Heather, Fiori Berhane, Daniela Bleichmar, Rachel Clement-Tolley, Lisa Cooper Vest, Neil Dewar, Carla Gharibian, Louise Haywood, Nelson Lam, Isabelle McNeill, Leila Mukhida, Henry Stoll, and Gwenhivir Wyatt-Moon for their help and advice during the publishing process. I am grateful to Andrew Arthur, Daniel Atkinson, Tom Baarda, Catherine Groom, Holly Smith, and Kristiina Watt for recording some of the music discussed herein for my paper presented at the 2022 International Musicological Society conference. I appreciate the helpful feedback that I received from attendees at this IMS meeting; at the Royal College of Music *Music, Mobility, and Migration* conference; at the Cambridge Italian Research Network Symposium; at the University of California, Santa Barbara, Music Theory Forum; and at the USC Musicology Forum. Maurice Whitehead and the Reverend Dr. Stephen Wang at the Venerable English College generously welcomed me into their archives and community. This research was funded by the Harvard University Center for Italian Renaissance Studies; the Renaissance Society of America; the US-Italy Fulbright Commission; the Harvard University Graduate School of Arts and Sciences; the Harvard Department of Music Ferdinand Gordon and Elizabeth Hunter Morrill Graduate Fellowship; the Paul and Andrew W. Mellon Rome Prize in Renaissance and Early Modern Studies; the Thole Research Fellowship in Music at Trinity Hall, Cambridge; and the USC Society of Fellows in the Humanities.

Cambridge Elements

Music, 1600–1750

Rebecca Herissone
University of Manchester

Rebecca Herissone is Professor of Musicology at the University of Manchester and a Fellow of the British Academy. She is also a Vice-President of the Royal Musical Association, Chair of the Musica Britannica Editorial Committee and a member of several Editorial Boards. Her research focuses on the music of early modern England, particularly issues of creativity, material culture and reception. She has published three monographs, most recently the award-winning *Musical Creativity in Restoration England*, and articles in a wide range of international journals. She is currently working towards an interdisciplinary study of the material traces of Purcell's reception.

Daniel R. Melamed
Indiana University (Emeritus)

Daniel R. Melamed is professor emeritus of musicology at the Indiana University Jacobs School of Music and director of the Bloomington Bach Cantata Project. He has served as editor of the Journal of Musicology and president of the American Bach Society. With Michael Marissen he is the creator of BachCantataTexts.org, a free source of historically informed translations for the music of J. S. Bach. His books include *J. S. Bach and the German Motet*, *Hearing Bach's Passions*, and *Listening to Bach: The Mass in B Minor and the Christmas Oratorio*.

About the Series

This series offers new perspectives on how music was created, performed, heard and understood within the rich and vibrant cultures of the seventeenth and early eighteenth centuries. Cutting across national boundaries and genre distinctions, it explores both professional and recreational music-making in a wide range of social and geographical contexts.

Cambridge Elements

Music, 1600–1750

Elements in the Series

Lettera amorosa: Musical Love Letters in Early Modern Italy
Roseen Giles

English Madrigals on the Jesuit Stage: Musical Theatre of Martyrdom at the Venerable English College, Rome
Alana Mailes

A full series listing is available at: www.cambridge.org/EMSE

For EU product safety concerns, contact us at Calle de José Abascal, 56–1°, 28003 Madrid, Spain or eugpsr@cambridge.org.

www.ingramcontent.com/pod-product-compliance
Ingram Content Group UK Ltd.
Pitfield, Milton Keynes, MK11 3LW, UK
UKHW022240230426

12048UKWH00018BA/1382